PREPARING
CHILDREN FOR
READING SUCCESS

PREPARING CHILDREN FOR READING SUCCESS

HANDS-ON ACTIVITIES FOR LIBRARIANS, EDUCATORS, AND CAREGIVERS

Julia Irwin and Dina Moore

ROWMAN & LITTLEFIELD
Lanham • Boulder • New York • London

Published by Rowman & Littlefield
A wholly owned subsidiary of The Rowman & Littlefield Publishing Group, Inc.
4501 Forbes Boulevard, Suite 200, Lanham, Maryland 20706
www.rowman.com

16 Carlisle Street, London W1D 3BT, United Kingdom

British Library Cataloguing in Publication Information Available

Library of Congress Cataloging-in-Publication Data

Irwin, Julia, 1964–
  Preparing children for reading success : hands-on activities for librarians, educators, and caregivers / Julia Irwin and Dina Moore.
    pages cm
  Includes bibliographical references and index.
  ISBN 978-0-8108-9319-1 (cloth : alk. paper) — ISBN 978-0-8108-9253-8 (pbk. : alk. paper) — ISBN 978-0-8108-9254-5 (ebook) 1. Reading. 2. Literacy. 3. Children—Books and reading. 4. Creative activities and seat work. I. Moore, Dina, 1972- II. Title.
  LB1050.I784 2014
  428.4—dc23   2014024514

♾™ The paper used in this publication meets the minimum requirements of American National Standard for Information Sciences—Permanence of Paper for Printed Library Materials, ANSI/NISO Z39.48-1992.

States of America

In memory of our colleague and mentor Anne E. Fowler

Anne's scientific work on early literacy and her creative ideas for how to translate the science into hands-on activities appropriate for use with very young children was the foundation for this book. Her tireless efforts during her too-brief lifetime to find ways to best ensure that children learn to read inspired us to write the book. Through teaching and mentoring us, the seeds of literacy that Anne planted will be sown through all the caregivers, educators, and librarians who pick it up, and most importantly, in the children in whom they instill a love for reading.

CONTENTS

FOREWORD

This book is a fitting tribute to Anne E. Fowler, who touched many lives by her groundbreaking studies of children's cognition and language, especially her penetrating research at Haskins Laboratories on the precursors of reading and writing and the all-important first steps. The goal of her unremitting efforts to improve the teaching of reading was nothing less than to ensure that children everywhere succeed in acquiring those precious literacy skills that are the indispensable foundation of further education.

This book is written in that spirit. The authors give wise guidance to parents and other caregivers, showing how to provide young children with the experiences and skills that will enable them learn to read in a timely manner and enable them to benefit fully from school-based instruction. This book explains how literacy builds on spoken language experiences and skills. Some preliterate language skills, for example, awareness that words are made up of consonant and vowel segments, can and should be explicitly taught. For building vocabulary and for promoting active understanding, it is vitally important for caregivers to engage children in give-and-take conversation. Adults can promote comprehension of the language of books by reading to and with children, and by engaging them in discussion of the content. The significant adults in a child's life can show best by their example that reading is a valued activity: children should see adults reading and enjoying books.

The authors' recommendations are thoroughly practical. They spared no effort to find supporting activities that will engage a child's interest at each of the successive steps toward achieving literacy. These activities are appealing to children and easy for parents and other adults to implement. In addition, the authors provide valuable suggestions for further reading about aspects of literacy and their instruction.

Donald Shankweiler
Senior Scientist, Haskins Laboratories, New Haven, Connecticut
Professor Emeritus, University of Connecticut,
Department of Psychology, Storrs, Connecticut

PREFACE

*P*reparing Children for Reading Success: Hands-On Activities for Librarians, Educators, and Caregivers is designed to familiarize you with the information that you need to prepare the child in your life to learn to read. By presenting the important elements in learning to read, we assist you in taking an active role to engage in behaviors that support literacy. We provide hands-on, real-world activities that you can do with a child or group of children to support emerging literacy. We also suggest specific titles of children's books to share with your child to support the activities that we present. In addition, we alert you to behaviors that may indicate risk for later problems with reading.

Caregivers (including parents, grandparents, siblings, child-care providers), preschool educators, librarians, or anyone else involved in the care of children will benefit from this book.

For each of these chapters, we provide a detailed description of the concepts and background research on the importance of this particular element in learning to read and suggest hands-on activities for engaging children with the concept. Additionally, we provide a list of children's books that you can use to demonstrate each of the concepts discussed.

The content was developed based on research on early literacy and what is known to be effective in promoting emerging reading development. We take these skills and suggest real-world activities and ideas to engage your child with language, reading, and print.

In addition to the more traditional discussion of topics important to learning to read (such as alphabet knowledge), this book includes a chapter on the social-emotional aspects of reading to children, an important part of both a child's emotional and cognitive development.

We provide step-by-step descriptions of activities to do with a child or group of children to support emerging literacy. In addition, we pair our suggestions for specific children's books to complete these activities and give the reader guidance for what kinds of books would be good for each activity.

A crucial skill that we hope to instill in parents and caregivers is the confidence and knowledge to engage their children in reading. In addition, we want to expose caregivers to the "hidden" elements crucial to early literacy, such as building a rich vocabulary before your child is ready to learn to read.

ORGANIZATION

Chapter 1, "The Importance of Reading," considers one of the most crucial achievements for a young child—learning to read. We discuss the elements that support learning to read, and outline the average course of reading development, from infancy through school age. We also examine the dire consequences of when a child falls behind in reading. Finally, we introduce how to support early literacy as a parent, librarian, teacher, or caregiver and set the stage for the chapters that follow.

"The Social-Emotional Benefits of Reading," chapter 2, focuses on the social-emotional, attentional, and self-regulation skills that underlie success in learning to read and in an educational setting more broadly. The ability to manage emotions, to pay attention to new and sometimes difficult material, and to persist with challenges are all crucial for success in an academic setting. In this chapter, we encourage caregivers, teachers, and librarians to use books as a tool for introducing vocabulary, increasing joint attention, and encouraging a love of books. From the earliest ages, books can be part of a caregiving repertoire, to calm down before a nap or bedtime, to provide one-on-one time with a parent or grandparent, or to signal quiet time at preschool or at the library. In addition, books can provide a valuable opportunity for difficult discussions about emotional topics, such as bullying, loneliness, or the death of a pet.

Taking a sequential approach, we first introduce alphabet knowledge (chapter 3) as part of a specific set of skills needed to support early literacy. This chapter highlights the importance of the alphabet, the building blocks of words. In this chapter, we give librarians, teachers, and caregivers advice about the right types of books to choose to illustrate the alphabet and provide a number of activities to teach children about the alphabet in engaging ways.

Our examination of skills continues with chapter 4, "Book-Handling Skills and Concepts about Print." Knowing about books and how they work is crucial for an emergent reader. It is easy to teach a child how to properly hold a book, the front from the back of the book, and that text (at least in English) reads from left to right. More difficult is to teach children that words on the page are written versions of what is said, and the difference between words, pictures, and numbers in the book. These concepts about print are crucial in understanding speech-to-print matching, and in this chapter we help you with activities that allow children to understand that a given spoken word in a book has a related printed form.

Chapter 5, "Phonological Awareness," presents another set of critical skills for learning to read (including attention to the sounds of the language, rhyming, and alliteration). In this chapter we present what phonological awareness is and why it is necessary. We then provide general principles to keep in mind when introducing phonological awareness. Finally, we convey a set of activities to strengthen these crucial skills.

Chapter 6 explores why vocabulary is important for reading and discusses how children come to acquire vocabulary. Books are an outstanding way to expose children to new words. We provide information about what types of words are a good fit for young children of different ages. This chapter also provides activities for building vocabulary with children.

Decontextualized language is the focus of chapter 7. Decontextualized language refers to understanding words without the support of context or pictures. The goal of this chapter is to move children toward using and understanding the more precise and complex language used in the classroom.

Writing and reading go hand in hand. There are many good reasons to write with young children. While reading is taking the printed word and converting it to sounds, writing is taking the sounds and converting them to the printed word. In this manner, reading and writing together can fuel emerging literacy. In chapter 8 we provide activities that support writing and discuss developmentally appropriate skills in these areas.

Literacy is a crucial achievement in the life of a child. It is necessary to ensure its success because so much else hinges on it. In this book you will discover skills important to learning to read and techniques that you can use to support these skills. These practices, while grounded in scientific research, are accessible and easy to implement by parents, caregivers, librarians, and teachers. In addition to arming you with this crucial information, we also hope that you will discover the joy of reading to a child and the thrill of later watching that same child learn to read independently. From its beginnings in the sounds that infants babble to children learning to decode and comprehend text, learning to read is an amazing and sometimes difficult process. Reading launches a child into a world filled with words, stories, and knowledge. *Preparing Children for Reading Success: Hands-On Activities for Librarians, Educators, and Caregivers* will help you learn how to create a reader, and by doing so, create a lifelong learner.

ACKNOWLEDGMENTS

This book is based partially on an article originally published in *Children and Libraries*, the journal of the Association for Library Service to Children. We are grateful to *Children and Libraries* for publishing this work.

INTRODUCTION

The development of good reading and writing skills is essential for success in the modern world. Failure to develop age-appropriate literacy in childhood has been shown, time and time again, to negatively impact social-emotional, educational, and economic outcomes as children transition into adulthood. To say that we have a literacy crisis in the United States is an understatement. Large percentages of children in all sectors of our society are not reading on grade level. This state of affairs should be unacceptable to all of us, especially because much is known on how to fix this problem. Indeed, there is a great deal of evidence in place on how children learn to read, what tends to go wrong when reading is problematic, and most importantly, how to begin to fix things early on with evidence-based approaches to instruction and remediation. The importance of addressing literacy gaps as early as possible cannot be overstated. In this volume the authors have provided an authoritative, but nontechnical, overview on each of these topics written for parents, librarians, and teachers alike.

Extensive evidence, from both cognitive studies and, more recently, from brain-imaging research shows that good literacy outcomes depend, in part, on early (preschool) language experiences. The development of good oral language skills in the first three years, a home environment that supports a developing love of books, enriched oral vocabulary, and exercises that reinforce the appreciation of the phonological characteristics of spoken words are all critical in preparing the child to master basic decoding skills in school. The relevant evidence, along with hands-on recommendations on how to promote good preliteracy readiness, is presented in the early chapters. The importance of social-emotional factors, along with enriched language stimulation, for good reading outcomes is also clearly discussed in the initial chapters. The parent and caregiver is, of course, a child's first (and most important) teacher; knowing what works and what doesn't in preparing the child to eventually learn literate language is something that all of us need to educate ourselves about.

Once children begin formal literacy instruction in school, overwhelming evidence shows that good instruction must include a strong focus on the basics of how spoken and written language are related to one another. This basic understanding does not occur spontaneously in most children, and problems in developing this understanding are almost always a core problem in children with reading struggles. Direct instruction on print-speech relationships is a crucial component of both good instruction and appropriate remediation. Constructs like phonological awareness, the alphabetic principle, letter-sound decoding, print vocabulary, and lexical quality are key elements in this process, and they are carefully presented in this book.

Finally, once the core elements are learned, and appropriate brain connections that support fluent decoding are established, good reading habits are essential to strengthen the system going forward. Importantly, we need to attend to what the child needs as the child transitions from "learning to read" to "reading to learn." A focus on strategies for comprehension becomes relevant to keep children on the right track. A premium on expressive skills (writing) becomes particularly salient at this point and is clearly discussed in later chapters of the book.

In summary, much is known about teaching and remediation in the domain of literacy. It is critical given what can only be described as a national reading crisis, that evidence-based practices are available to stakeholders. This book does a terrific job of meeting the challenge of translating "research to practice" and should become an invaluable resource to parents, librarians, and educators.

Ken Pugh
Director, Yale University Reading Center, New Haven, Connecticut
President, Director of Research and Senior Scientist,
Haskins Laboratories, New Haven, Connecticut

1

THE IMPORTANCE OF READING

Once you learn to read, you will be forever free.

—Frederick Douglass

WHY IS READING IMPORTANT?

One of the most important academic achievements for a young child is learning to read. The National Association for the Education of Young Children states that "one of the best predictors of whether a child will function competently in school and go on to contribute in an increasingly literate society is the level to which the child progresses in reading and writing" (Neuman, Copple, and Bredekamp, 1999, 3). So how do we help our children become proficient readers? Many of us are surprised and awed by how quickly and effortlessly most children learn how to speak, and we assume that learning to read should be as simple. Based on this assumption, we would expect that children would learn to read with exposure to books and a print-rich environment. However, while many children show an interest in books and storytelling early on, most children do not learn to read without *some* instruction. In fact, contrary to what many people believe (including many educators), children do not learn to read "naturally." Learning to read and write is quite different from learning to speak and listen and requires careful planning and instruction (Snow, Burns, and Griffin, 1998). Therefore, we need to provide early readers an effective, explicit introduction to reading. Because learning to read is so critical to a child's development and future, we cannot leave it up to chance.

WHAT ARE THE ELEMENTS THAT SUPPORT LEARNING TO READ?

As adults, it is difficult to remember that becoming a skilled reader is an incredibly complex task. Skilled reading requires quick and accurate word recognition in order to successfully comprehend text. While young children are learning to decode (i.e., to successfully sound out words), they also must access their knowledge of language, vocabulary, and the world around them to be able to understand what they are reading (Scarborough, 2001). Because reading is so complex and the development of skilled reading so critical, there are many techniques and approaches that have been used to help children learn to read. However, while many of these approaches have been grounded in good intentions, they have not always been scientifically tested to see whether they are successful (Lyon, Shaywitz, Shaywitz, and Chhabra, 2005; Moats, 1999). Because of this, we believe that it is crucial to draw from evidence- or research-based practice to realize what works in early literacy. Fortunately, the current research on early literacy instruction has provided the information necessary to successfully promote this emerging skill in young children.

Several special panels have convened to address the issue of literacy in children, focusing in part on the elements that are precursors for later literacy. These panels include the National Research Council (Snow, Burns, and Griffin, 1998), National Reading Panel (National Institute of Child Health and Human Development, 2000), and the National Early Literacy Panel (National Early Literacy Panel, 2008). The results of these panels provide overlapping support for a common set of skills important for literacy development.

A central conclusion from these expert panels focusing on literacy is that *spoken* language provides a critical foundation for reading. Familiarity with spoken language is crucial, and children vary dramatically in the amount of vocabulary words that they know when they begin to learn to read. Children who enter school with lower vocabulary tend to hear fewer words and fewer different words, hear more commands (e.g., "Sit down") rather than prompts and questions, and have less overall interaction with adults (Hart and Risley, 1995). Thus, we want to promote language expression—that is, to enhance spoken language in children to prepare them to learn to read. After all, how can a child recognize and learn to read words in print if he has never heard those words before? To support early spoken (or oral) language development, you can simply engage in many of the activities that you already do with young children, such as singing, using fingerplay (hand action or movement combined with singing or spoken words, such as the Itsy Bitsy Spider, which uses singing, rhyming, and fingerplay) and rhymes, talking, *and* reading. To create an environment that supports spoken language once your child begins to talk, it is important to speak and listen to children, to engage in responsive interactions with plenty of time for the child to respond. In addition, the use of varied, rich vocabulary will introduce children to new words.

A second major conclusion from the expert panels is that intentional, explicit instruction of certain skills will facilitate learning to read (Scarborough, 2001; Snow, Burns, and Griffin, 1998). By intentional, we mean that activities and books are planned in advance to meet some specific goal. Choices are guided by what children know and by where you want to take them. We will demonstrate this in future chapters as we discuss picking out questions to ask in advance when reading stories or in choosing vocabulary words to introduce. In the following chapters, we will present evidence-based techniques that are the basis of effective literacy instruction. To make these principles accessible, we have grounded them in everyday activities and practices that you can adopt and use with the child in your life.

WHAT IS THE AVERAGE COURSE OF READING DEVELOPMENT?

Because reading is so complex, we cannot expect that children will become readers overnight. Many of the early precursors to skilled reading emerge not just from literacy development, but also from the child's oral language development. What follows are some developmental highlights and im-portant milestones in oral language and literacy development (summarized from a number of expert sources in this area) to help guide you in knowing what to expect at different points in child development (Chall, 1983; Snow, Burns, and Griffin, 1998; Torgesen and Mathes, 2000).

First Year

Within the first year of life, caregivers witness many important language milestones. From very early on, infants are able to perceive the sounds of the language being spoken around them. In fact, evidence indicates that infants are able to perceive differences in many speech sounds across languages and quickly learn to distinguish the sounds of their native language. Evidence also suggests that from soon after birth infants can recognize the sound of their mothers' voices and show a preference for her voice over other female voices. While the ability to understand the spoken word at first outpaces the ability to produce words, most infants begin saying their first words around the time of their first birthday.

Many infants enjoy shared book reading and show an early interest in board books and simple stories. Young infants may not be capable of holding books and looking at them in the same way as older children, and in fact may spend a lot of time banging, throwing, and mouthing the books. However, children who are read to regularly will begin to show their understanding of how books function by beginning to turn the pages, holding the book right side up, and babbling or making other sounds as they turn the pages.

Two to Three Years

The second year of life brings a huge increase in the size of the child's productive vocabulary (i.e., the number of words the child can say). We also see the beginning of two- to three-word sentences during this time, with increases in sentence complexity by the time children reach age three.

Children may begin to "read" familiar stories as they are looking at books. This can include using a "storytelling"-like style and intonation as they describe the pages or even retelling parts of books that have been read to them frequently. Children may also show an increasing awareness of the function of books by holding them correctly and turning the pages starting from the front of the book to the back. At this age, some children may become interested in writing and pretend to read the scribbles that they have written. As they get closer to age three, the scribbles may begin to look more like letters.

By this age children may begin to have some sensitivity to the sounds of words, a very important precursor to literacy. Specifically, some children evidence an ability to detect the rhyming nature of words. As we will discuss later, the awareness of the sounds of spoken language (*phonological awareness*) is an important precursor to reading development.

Three to Four Years

Children at this age can identify approximately ten letters and recognize what is print and what is not. Children are beginning to scribble in a way that looks more like actual letters and may include some random letters within the scribbles they make. As they get closer to age four, some children may even be able to write highly familiar words and spell the beginning sounds of some words. Children may also "read" books to themselves, illustrating the development of *concepts about print*. This is an understanding that the words on the page are telling the story, rather than the drawings, and that print is read from the left to right, and the top of the page to the bottom of the page.

In addition, three- to four-year-old children are beginning to show an interest in language play, including *rhyming* and *alliteration* (knowing the beginning sounds of words, for example, that mouse and man both begin with *m*).

Four to Five Years

As children approach kindergarten, most can name letters of the alphabet, recognize some signs (e.g., street signs), and may be able to recognize their own name in print and even write their own name. When children begin kindergarten, they continue to show increased sensitivity to the sounds of their language. For example, they may be able to indicate whether two words rhyme and may generate a rhyme for a simple word. Toward the end of kindergarten, we see further development in the ability to manipulate the sounds in spoken words with skills such as the ability to isolate and pronounce the beginning sounds of words and beginning ability in blending sounds. These *phonological awareness* skills will continue to develop and become more sophisticated throughout kindergarten and first grade. Importantly, the child's vocabulary (the words that the child knows and recognizes) will continue to be important as he or she is beginning to match these words with letters and sounds.

Six to Seven Years

For most children, first grade is when they become real readers. This is the time when children begin to learn the relationships between written letters and the sounds those letters make. In this early reading stage, children are able to read simple texts that contain words that are easy to pronounce and are highly familiar. First graders may also be able to use some of their new decoding skills to sound out simple unfamiliar words.

Seven to Eight Years

By seven to eight years (approximately second grade) children can read increasingly more complex stories with much more *fluency*. Fluency refers to reading that becomes smoother and more automatic, with an increase in the words that children can recognize quickly by sight.

Nine to Thirteen Years

During this stage we see that children become increasingly more competent readers, with the ability to read more complex and novel texts. Children have quickly moved from the early stages of learning to read and into the stage of reading to learn. Note that at this age, most of children's learning is via text. This learning may be done through fiction books and articles, and perhaps even more through nonfiction sources, such as textbooks, articles, and websites.

WHAT HAPPENS IF A CHILD FALLS BEHIND?

The importance of effective *early* exposure to literacy cannot be emphasized enough. Unfortunately, many children are already behind when they enter kindergarten. Sobering evidence from multiple sources indicates that children who fall behind in reading acquisition do not catch up (Francis, Shaywitz, Shaywitz, Steubing, and Fletcher, 1996; Juel, 1988; Torgesen and Burgess, 1998). Children who fall behind in first grade have a one-in-eight chance of ever catching up to grade level without extraordinary intervention efforts (Juel, 1988). Further, children who fall behind in reading at seven years of age continue to lag behind at age twelve and beyond (Francis, Shaywitz, Shaywitz, Steubing, and Fletcher, 1996). In the classic model known as the Matthew effect, Keith Stanovich states that early lags in literacy become magnified with reading development (Stanovich, 1986). Specifically, the Matthew effect shows the "rich get richer" (in this case, good readers become more fluent and effective), and the "poor get poorer" (poor readers fall further and further behind). This phenomenon has been observed in research examining how new readers acquire the skills to read: early success in acquiring reading skills typically leads to later successes in reading as the learner grows. Failing to learn to read before the third or fourth year of schooling may be indicative of lifelong problems in skills central to literacy (Scarborough, 1998). Further, children who fall behind in reading read less, increasing the gap between them and their peers. As children advance in school, text becomes increasingly difficult and students must "read to learn" (where before they were learning to read). Their reading difficulties then create deficits in most other subjects (Allington, 1984). Thus, research-to-practice efforts for a number of intervention programs focus on preliteracy skills.

WHAT CAN I DO TO SUPPORT LITERACY FOR THE CHILD IN MY LIFE?

We believe that small efforts early on will have a big payoff later for children as they acquire literacy. Based on what we know from studies of young kindergarteners, we have established that effective literacy instruction includes a number of important elements (Snow, Burns, and Griffin, 1998). First, effective literacy instruction is intentional. Again, this means that activities and books are planned in advance to meet a specific goal, such as choosing vocabulary words to focus upon when reading stories. The choices that you make in working with an individual child or a small group of children can be guided by what the children already know (which you can ascertain based on your interactions with them). To be effective, it is important to decide explicitly what the information is the child should learn, to model the desired activity or skill, and to provide the opportunity for the child to try it out and give feedback. Additionally, effective literacy instruction is both systematic and sequential. Together these terms refer to the fact that instruction must build from what is known to what is new, presenting developmentally appropriate (those that can be grasped by a child of a given age) concepts. For example, an emphasis on how to hold a book (book handling) is more appropriate for a group of two- and three-year-olds, while introducing alliteration (repetition of an initial consonant sound) might be better suited to four- and five-year-olds. The activities and books chosen should be interesting in order to fully engage children so they enjoy learning. Additionally, concepts should be reinforced with ample practice. Children love to do things over and over (including reading a favorite book). Hands-on practice with concrete materials, such as an easel for writing, manipulatives (for example, foam models of the alphabet and magnetic alphabet shapes), and access to previously read books facilitates this practice. Finally, in every activity, it is important to involve all of the child's modes of interacting. When hearing a story, children should be not always just listening, but speaking and "reading" (which may be following along by pointing to words as you read them).

Finally, to support emerging literacy, it is also crucial to remember to provide a "literate" environment (Neuman, Copple, and Bredekamp, 1999, 3). This can be done by having interesting books and other reading materials available to children, by creating a comfortable area for reading, by labeling objects with print, by pointing out and answering questions about print in the child's surroundings (such as on signs, advertisements, or menus) and, finally, to let the child or children in your life see you reading.

In summary, the current research on early literacy instruction has provided the information necessary to successfully promote emerging literacy in young children. In the following chapters, we will explore each of the identified key preliteracy skills that prepare young children for reading success. These skills include alphabet knowledge (chapter 3), concepts about print (chapter 4), phonological awareness (chapter 5), expressive vocabulary (chapter 6), decontextualized language (chapter 7), and writing with your child (chapter 8). For each identified skill, we provide suggestions for developmentally appropriate children's books and lay out activities to illustrate each concept.

REFERENCES

Allington, Richard. "Content Coverage and Contextual Reading in Reading Groups." *Journal of Reading Behavior* 16, no. 2 (1984): 85–96.

Chall, Jeanne S. *Stages of Reading Development.* New York: McGraw-Hill, 1983.

Francis, David, Sally Shaywitz, Bennett Shaywitz, Karla Steubing, and Jack Fletcher. "Developmental Lag versus Deficit Models of Reading Disability: A Longitudinal, Individual Growth Curves Analysis." *Journal of Educational Psychology* 88, no. 1 (1996): 3–17.

Hart, Betty, and Todd Risley. *Meaningful Differences in the Everyday Experiences of Young American Children.* New York: Paul H. Brooks, 1995.

Juel, Connie. "Learning to Read and Write: A Longitudinal Study of 54 Children from the First through Fourth Grades." *Journal of Educational Psychology* 80, no. 4 (1988): 437–47.

Lyon, G. Reid, Sally Shaywitz, Bennett Shaywitz, and Vinita Chhabra. *Evidence-Based Reading Policy in the United States: How Scientific Research Informs Instructional Practices.* Washington, D.C.: Brookings Institution Press, 2005.

Moats, Louisa. *Teaching Reading Is Rocket Science: What Expert Teachers of Reading Should Know and Be Able to Do.* Washington, D.C.: American Federation of Teachers, 1999.

National Early Literacy Panel. *Developing Early Literacy: Report of the National Early Literacy Panel.* Washington, D.C.: National Institute for Literacy, 2008.

National Institute of Child Health and Human Development. *Teaching Children to Read: An Evidence-Based Assessment of the Scientific Research Literature on Reading and Its Implications for Reading Instruction. Report of the National Reading Panel.* Washington, D.C.: U.S. Government Printing Office, 2000.

Neuman, Susan B., Carol Copple, and Susan Bredekamp. *Learning to Read and Write: Developmentally Appropriate Practices for Young Children.* Washington, D.C.: NAEYC, 1999.

Scarborough, Hollis. "Connecting Early Language and Literacy to Later Reading (Dis)abilities: Evidence, Theory, and Practice." In *Handbook of Early Literacy Research*, edited by Susan B. Neuman and David K. Dickinson. New York: Guilford, 2001.

———. "Early Identification of Children at Risk for Reading Disabilities: Phonological Awareness and Some Other Promising Predictors." *In Specific Reading Disability: A View of the Spectrum*, edited by Bruce K. Shapiro, Pasquale J. Accardo, and Arnold J. Capute, 75–119. Timonium, Md.: York, 1998.

Snow, Catherine, M. Susan Burns, and Peg Griffin. *Preventing Reading Difficulties in Young Children.* Washington, D.C.: National Research Council, National Academy Press, 1998.

Stanovich, Keith. "Matthew Effects in Reading: Some Consequences of Individual Differences in the Acquisition of Literacy." *Reading Research Quarterly* 21, no. 4 (1986): 360–406.

Torgesen, Joseph K., and Stephen R. Burgess. "Consistency of Reading-Related Phonological Processes throughout Early Childhood: Evidence From Longitudinal-Correlational and Instructional Studies." In *Word Recognition in Beginning Literacy*, edited by Jamie Metsala and Linnea Ehri. Hillsdale, N.J.: Erlbaum, 1998.

Torgesen, Joseph K., and Patricia G. Mathes. *A Basic Guide to Understanding, Assessing, and Teaching Phonological Awareness.* Austin, Tex.: Pro-Ed, 2000.

2

THE SOCIAL-EMOTIONAL BENEFITS OF READING

Children are made readers on the laps of their parents.

—Emilie Buchwald

Along with the skills targeted toward literacy, it is also important to know that children must acquire the social-emotional, attentional, and self-regulation skills necessary to interact with others, to have an interest in learning to read, and to be able to persist with new and sometimes difficult material in school (Dickinson, McCabe, and Essex, 2006). The earliest experiences that support literacy in children, including nursery rhymes, fingerplay, songs, conversations, and book reading (Landry and Smith, 2006) are an excellent way for caregivers to both share social-emotional interactions with their children (Newson, 2006) *and* a way to begin preparing their child to read (Landry and Smith, 2006).

What many caregivers already know is that books provide a powerful opportunity to connect with the children in their lives from infancy through school age, and beyond. Books can be a central part of the social and emotional development of a child by creating occasions for sharing and engaging with others. Books encourage one-on-one time (or one on two, or three, depending on the number of children in your life) with a caregiver or teacher. Books give you a reason to turn off devices and media and share quiet time together with your child(ren) on your lap or by your side. Sensitive caregiving behaviors such as showing positive emotions, physical closeness, and appropriately modulated use of voice (e.g., soothing for a quiet bedtime book) all can be carried out while reading to the child in your life.

Responsive caregiving includes behaviors that encourage shared attention and engagement, which can be done in the context of reading a book (Landry and Smith, 2006). A key feature of social-emotional development that will ultimately support literacy and learning is joint attention, which refers to the social sharing of focus of two individuals on an object. A simple illustrative example of this might be a caregiver and young child at the zoo, where the caregiver gets the child's attention and points out some interesting object, such as a giraffe. In this manner, caregivers, teachers, librarians, parents, and grandparents focus a child's attention to some object, allowing it to be identified and labeled. Notably, joint attention creates a situation where children are focused on the items that their caregiver points out, an optimal situation for learning new words. Tomasello and Farrar (1986) report that during joint play the "conversations" (or interactions that include language) between the mother and child were longer when attention was shared and that new words were more readily learned in this context. Children can encounter new words through books, first by hearing the word, and when they are ready, by both hearing the word and seeing it in print. As a caregiver, you can foster joint attention using books by pointing out letters, words, or images in a book (depending on the developmental level of the child).

Another social-emotional skill that emerges from reading to a child is the ability to take turns when interacting with others. Devices such as television, computers, phones, and tablets typically provide immediate feedback and may not require the child to interact or respond (for example, when watching a video). We would argue that social reciprocity—the ability to listen to others, to take turns, and to negotiate with someone else—increases and supports social attention. While it may not be obvious that social reciprocity and attention is related to the ability to learn to read, these skills are critical for success in school.

Some practical examples of how to incorporate books in your everyday life to support both social and emotional development and emerging literacy include using books as a part of your caregiving routine, as a starting point for discussing difficult or emotional topics, and as a basis for activities to do with your child.

As an example of using books as a part of a caregiving routine, you may read a book every day after school, or before naps or at bedtime. Using books as a part of an evening ritual, for example, can lead to a calming transition that helps your child to settle and sleep. One book that has been used for generations by parents at bedtime is *Goodnight Moon* by Margaret Wise Brown. Toward the end of the story there is a passage that reads, "Goodnight stars, goodnight air, goodnight noises everywhere." For prereaders, you could substitute your own child's name to wish them good night (such as "Goodnight Joe, goodnight Claire, goodnight noises everywhere"). This personalizes the connection with the book, making the child feel as though the book is for her. Other good examples of soothing stories include *Kiss Good Night* by Amy Hest, *The Napping House* by Audrey Wood, or *On Mother's Lap* by Ann Herbert Scott.

Books are also a great way to share ideas and feelings. Books can allow you to start discussions about almost any topic: history, science, nature, or even concerns or fears. If your child approaches you with questions about a topic, you can find books to read together and discuss that topic in more detail. Books can help you to start a conversation about something difficult or emotional. For example, if you have recently lost a pet, a book like *Dog Heaven* by Cynthia Rylant can provide a starting point for talking with your child about your child's feelings about his or her loss. Or, if your child has jitters about the first day of school or day care, you could read *Curious George's First Day of School* by Margret and H. A. Rey, *The Hello, Goodbye Window* by Norton Juster, or *The Kissing Hand* by Audrey Penn and ask your child if he thinks his experience will be like the characters in the book(s). Discussing books together creates a time for your child to share his or her thoughts, worries, and ideas with you, to practice new words that he or she has learned from the book, and to discuss conflicts and concepts that arise in the book. For example, a couple of books that touch on teasing and feeling unloved or bullied that even very young children can understand are *Unlovable* by Dan Yaccarino or *Chrysanthemum* by Kevin Henkes. In *Wemberly Worried* by Kevin Henkes, the main character worries about everything, which children may relate to. *Being Friends* by Karen Beaumont is a book about friendship that emphasizes that people can be friends even if they are different from each other. By talking about the perspectives and feelings of favorite characters, children learn to better understand others' and their own feelings.

Reading books aloud is ideal for connecting children of all ages, from reading a board book to an infant on your lap to reading a series, such as the Harry Potter series by J. K. Rowling to older children a chapter at a time. The interactions and shared time continue to be important throughout your child's life. There are also a number of books that are designed to have you and your child take turns reading aloud to each other, such as *You Read to Me, I'll Read to You: Very Short Stories to Read Together* and *You Read to Me, I'll Read to You: Very Short Fables to Read Together,* both by Mary Ann Hoberman and Michael Emberley.

Books can also be the focus of activities to do with your young child. You can visit the library or bookstore with a child or group of children and have them pick out books that interest them. Following up on topics that you have read about provides great ideas for activities to do with children. For example, you could read the classic story *The Gingerbread Man* (one version is by Jim Aylesworth) and then bake gingerbread men at home, or bring them to day care or school. A book like *Make Way for Ducklings* by Robert McCloskey could be a starting point for a trip to the local park to see the ducks. A book about the human body (such as *My First Human Body Book* by Donald Silver and Patricia Wynne) could help prepare a child for a trip to a science museum. James Mayhew has a series of books that introduce children to fine art through a young girl named Katie. This series is an excellent example of books to read before you visit an art museum with your child (for example, see *Katie's Sunday Afternoon*, *Katie and the Sunflowers*, *Katie and the Starry Night*, *Katie Meets the Impressionists*, all by James Mayhew).

Finally, demonstrating that reading is valued is crucially important, particularly with all of the competition for a child's time and attention (such as TV, computers, and tablets). Introducing children to books early, and often, will encourage them to view reading as a positive and pleasurable experience that they can continue to enjoy for the rest of their lives. Children will learn the purpose and functions of literacy and learn to place value on reading by observation, watching you read (books, magazines, or on the Internet) and having you read to them. To ensure a literate society, we need to produce readers. Children who like to read will read more. The skills that we highlight in this book set the stage for later success, producing a child that not just learns to read, but can read to learn.

RECOMMENDED BOOKS FOR SOCIAL-EMOTIONAL DEVELOPMENT

The Gingerbread Man	Jim Aylesworth
When Sophie Gets Angry—Really, Really Angry	Molly Bang
Being Friends	Karen Beaumont
Goodnight Moon	Margaret Wise Brown
The Way I Feel	Janan Cain
How Are You Peeling?	Saxton Freymann and Joost Elffers
Chrysanthemum	Kevin Henkes
Wemberly Worried	Kevin Henkes
Kiss Good Night	Amy Hest
You Read to Me, I'll Read to You: Very Short Fables to Read Together	Mary Ann Hoberman

You Read to Me, I'll Read to You: Very Short Stories to Read Together	Mary Ann Hoberman
The Hello, Goodbye Window	Norton Juster
The Circus Is Coming	Hilary Knight
Katie and the Starry Night	James Mayhew
Katie and the Sunflowers	James Mayhew
Katie Meets the Impressionists	James Mayhew
Katie's Sunday Afternoon	James Mayhew
Make Way for Ducklings	Robert McCloskey
The Feelings Book	Todd Parr
The Kissing Hand	Audrey Penn
Curious George's First Day of School	Margret and H. A. Rey
Harry Potter and the Chamber of Secrets	J. K. Rowling
Harry Potter and the Deathly Hallows	J. K. Rowling
Harry Potter and the Goblet of Fire	J. K. Rowling
Harry Potter and the Half-Blood Prince	J. K. Rowling
Harry Potter and the Order of the Phoenix	J. K. Rowling
Harry Potter and the Prisoner of Azkaban	J. K. Rowling
Harry Potter and the Sorcerer's Stone	J. K. Rowling
Dog Heaven	Cynthia Rylant
On Mother's Lap	Ann Herbert Scott
My Many Colored Days	Dr. Seuss
Welcome to the World	Nancy Elizabeth Wallace
The Pigeon Has Feelings, Too!	Mo Willems
The Napping House	Audrey Wood
My First Human Body Book	Donald Silver and Patricia Wynne
Unlovable	Dan Yaccarino

HOW-TO ACTIVITY: Fostering Joint Attention Using Books

Joint attention refers to the shared focus between two individuals on an object, in this case, a book. As we have described in this chapter, joint attention is a critical skill for both emergent literacy and for social and emotional development.

Behaviors that foster joint attention during reading include eye gaze, pointing, and language (often together!) to engage your child and bring his or her attention to objects in the book. For example, when reading a book, you can look to your child's face to gain his or her attention and then look toward the book that you are sharing. Even very young children will follow a point to specific images in a book.

If the child does not follow gaze, or if you are reading to a group of children, pointing will help to draw and maintain joint attention.

A sample book for a very young child or infant is *Welcome to the World* by Nancy Elizabeth Wallace. Using this book, you could gain your child's attention, then look toward the book and talk to your child about what you see ("Look, I see a bear!"). Another book for slightly older children that includes brightly colored images is *The Circus Is Coming* by Hilary Knight.

Sharing attention to images in books supports learning of new words and objects and provides an opportunity for sharing experiences together.

HOW-TO ACTIVITY: Discussing Emotions Using Books

In this chapter, we indicate that books provide an opportunity to discuss emotional or sensitive topics. The ability to identify one's own emotions and label emotions of others is a helpful skill, and books can support a child's ability to do so. Some titles that can be helpful with this include *How Are You Peeling?* by Saxton Freymann and Joost Elffers, *The Way I Feel* by Janan Cain, *When Sophie Gets Angry—Really, Really Angry* by Molly Bang, *The Feelings Book* by Todd Parr, *The Pigeon Has Feelings, Too!* by Mo Willems, or *My Many Colored Days* by Dr. Seuss. Using any of these titles, you could ask a child, "How is Sophie feeling?" "Do you ever feel that way?" An additional follow-up activity could be having a child draw a picture of how the child or a favorite character in a book is feeling. With *My Many Colored Days* you could have children explore feelings by using different colors of crayons, paints, paper, or any other art supply they are interested in.

HOW-TO ACTIVITY: Book Time

In this chapter, we suggested including books as part of a child's ritual, such as bedtime or nap time. In this way, the book becomes a tool for calming and soothing your child to get him or her ready for rest.

Another approach, if nap time or bedtime is not a good fit for reading, is to set aside "book time." Book time can be any time when devices are turned off, where your primary focus is reading to your child. Scheduling book time ensures that you make time for this activity and sends a message that books are valued. Important to social-emotional development is warm, close physical contact. We suggest, then, that book time is a time where your child sits on your lap or close by. If you are working with a group of children in a professional setting, you can have children sit in a circle around you while you read.

Any book can be chosen for book time, and allowing your child to select books can be an exciting and fun part of the process. Creating your own book with your child, about your child (e.g., including photographs of your child with text that you create together) can also be a wonderful way to engage your child and reinforce the child's sense of self. For a group, you could take turns reading books about each child that they have created.

REFERENCES

Dickinson, David K., Allyssa McCabe, and Marilyn J. Essex. "The Influence of Parenting on Emerging Literacy Skills." In *Handbook of Early Literacy Research*, vol. 2, edited by David K. Dickinson and Susan B. Neuman. New York: Guilford, 2006.

Landry, Susan, and Karen Smith. "The Influence of Parenting on Emerging Literacy Skills." In *Handbook of Early Literacy Research*, vol. 2, edited by David K. Dickinson and Susan B. Neuman. New York: Guilford, 2006.

Newson, John. "The Growth of Shared Understandings between Infant and Caregiver." In *Before Speech: The Beginnings of Interpersonal Communication*, edited by Margaret Bullowa. Cambridge, UK: Cambridge University Press, 2006.

Tomasello, Michael, and Michael J. Farrar. "Joint Attention and Early Language." *Child Development* 57, no. 6 (1986): 1454–63.

BIBLIOGRAPHY

Aylesworth, Jim. *The Gingerbread Man*. Illus. by Barbara McClintock. New York: Scholastic, 1998. 32 p.

Bang, Molly. *When Sophie Gets Angry—Really, Really Angry*. Illus. by the author. New York: Scholastic, 2004. 40 p.

Beaumont, Karen. *Being Friends*. Illus. by Joy Allen. New York: Dial, 2002. 32 p.

Brown, Margaret Wise. *Goodnight Moon*. Illus. by Clement Hurd. New York: HarperCollins, 1947. 30 p.

Cain, Janan. *The Way I Feel*. Illus. by the author. Seattle: Parenting Press, 2000. 32 p.

Freymann, Saxton, and Joost Elffers. *How Are You Peeling?* Illus. by the authors. New York: Arthur A. Levine Books, 1999. 40 p.

Henkes, Kevin. *Chrysanthemum*. Illus. by the author. New York: Greenwillow, 1991. 32 p.

———. *Wemberly Worried*. Illus. by the author. New York: Greenwillow, 2000. 32 p.

Hest, Amy. *Kiss Good Night*. Illus. by Anita Jeram. Cambridge, Mass.: Candlewick, 2004. 30 p.

Hoberman, Mary Ann. *You Read to Me, I'll Read to You: Very Short Fables to Read Together*. Illus. by Michael Emberley. New York: Little, Brown, 2010. 32 p.

———. *You Read to Me, I'll Read to You: Very Short Stories to Read Together*. Illus. by Michael Emberley. New York: Little, Brown, 2009. 32 p.

Juster, Norton. *The Hello, Goodbye Window*. Illus. by Chris Raschka. New York: Hyperion, 2005. 32 p.

Knight, Hilary. *The Circus Is Coming*. Illus. by the author. New York: Golden Books, 2007. 56 p.

Mayhew, James. *Katie and the Starry Night*. Illus. by the author. London: Hodder & Stoughton, 2013. 32 p.

———. *Katie and the Sunflowers*. Illus. by the author. New York: Orchard, 2000. 32 p.

———. *Katie Meets the Impressionists*. Illus. by the author. New York: Orchard, 1997. 32 p.

——. *Katie's Sunday Afternoon*. Illus. by the author. New York: Orchard, 2004. 32 p.

McCloskey, Robert. *Make Way for Ducklings*. Illus. by the author. New York: Puffin, 1976. First published 1941 by Viking Press. 76 p.

Parr, Todd. *The Feelings Book*. Illus. by the author. New York: Little Brown and Company, 2000. 24 p.

Penn, Audrey. *The Kissing Hand*. Illus. by Ruth E. Harper and Nancy M. Leak. Terre Haute, Ind.: Tanglewood, 2006. 32 p.

Rey, Margaret, and H. A. Rey. *Curious George's First Day of School*. Illus. by Anna Grossnickle Hines. Boston: Houghton Mifflin, 2005. 24 p.

Rowling, J. K. *Harry Potter and the Chamber of Secrets*. Illus. by Mary Grandpre. New York: Scholastic, 1998. 341 p.

——. *Harry Potter and the Deathly Hallows*. Illus. by Mary Grandpre. New York: Scholastic, 2007. 759 p.

——. *Harry Potter and the Goblet of Fire*. Illus. by Mary Grandpre. New York: Scholastic, 2000. 734 p.

——. *Harry Potter and the Half-Blood Prince*. Illus. by Mary Grandpre. New York: Scholastic, 2005. 652 p.

——. *Harry Potter and the Order of the Phoenix*. Illus. by Mary Grandpre. New York: Scholastic, 2003. 870 p.

——. *Harry Potter and the Prisoner of Azkaban*. Illus. by Mary Grandpre. New York: Scholastic, 1999. 435 p.

——. *Harry Potter and the Sorcerer's Stone*. Illus. by Mary Grandpre. New York: Scholastic, 1997. 309 p.

Rylant, Cynthia. *Dog Heaven*. Illus. by the author. New York: Blue Sky, 1995. 40 p.

Scott, Ann Herbert. *On Mother's Lap*. Illus. by Glo Coalson. New York: Clarion, 1972. 32 p.

Seuss, Dr. *My Many Colored Days*. Illus. by Steve Johnson. New York: Alfred A. Knopf, 1996. 32 p.

Silver, Donald, and Patricia Wynne. *My First Human Body Book*. Mineola, N.Y.: Dover, 2009. 32 p.

Wallace, Nancy Elizabeth. *Welcome to the World*. Illus. by Marsela Hajadinjak-Krec. Branford, Conn.: Read to Grow. 20 p.

Willams, Mo. *The Pigeon Has Feelings, Too!* Illus. by the author. New York: Hyperion, 2005. 12 p.

Wood, Audrey. *The Napping House*. Illus. by Don Wood. New York: Harcourt, 1984. 32 p.

Yaccarino, Dan. *Unlovable*. New York: Holt, 2001. 32 p.

3

ALPHABET KNOWLEDGE

One of the greatest gifts adults can give—to their offspring and to their society—is to read to children.

—Carl Sagan

One skill essential to the acquisition of literacy is familiarity with the alphabet, or *alphabet knowledge*. Alphabet knowledge is the ability to visually recognize and name letters. Not surprisingly, research has shown that how well a child knows the alphabet at the beginning of kindergarten is a good predictor of later reading (Adams, 1994; Scarborough, 1998). Young children who know letters are likely to be those with the greatest exposure to books and print. While it is important to teach children these labels, the research is also very clear that teaching letters alone will not make a child a reader. However, alphabet knowledge is one important building block for young children. In keeping with the idea that we want to introduce skills sequentially, the initial emphasis with young children should be on identifying the letters visually. Once children can visually identify letters, then you can move on to emphasizing the sounds that the letters make. As children learn to recognize the letters, you can then encourage them to begin writing letters. In the following sections we introduce some books and activities that will emphasize alphabet knowledge for young children.

USING BOOKS TO TEACH ALPHABET KNOWLEDGE

There are countless books that focus on the letters of the alphabet. Many of these books can be read with children to familiarize them with letters. When first introducing children to alphabet books it is important to choose books that have a clear font and clear exemplars of the letters. One good example is *Flora McDonnell's ABC*, where the letters are introduced one at a time, and uppercase and lowercase are printed in a bold, bright, easy-to-read font. Some fonts are clear and easy to read, while others are less clear and may be difficult for young children. *ABeCedarios* by Cynthia Weill gives good examples of letters in both English and Spanish. Other books introduce letters using a rhythmic pattern and draw attention to the alphabet. For example, *Chicka Chicka Boom Boom* by Bill Martin Jr., John Archambault, and Lois Ehlert uses repetitive singsong phrasing to capture a young child's attention (e.g., "Whee!" said D to E F G, "I'll beat you to the top of the coconut tree").

When working with very young, emergent readers, it is also important to choose books that use one sound for each letter. This gives the child a clear example of what each letter sounds like (called sound-letter correspondence) and minimizes confusion. Some popular alphabet books useful to read at this stage are *Dr. Seuss's ABC* and *Eric Carle's ABC*. In the classic *Dr. Seuss's ABC* each letter is introduced one at a time (pairing uppercase and lowercase), and the rhythmic pattern of the book introduces the sounds of each of the letters. For example, "Big B, little b, what begins with B? Barber, baby, bubbles and a bumblebee." In addition, it is useful to vary selection between books emphasizing an alphabet song (e.g., *Chicka Chicka Boom Boom* by Bill Martin Jr., John Archambault, and Lois Ehlert) and those with strong exemplars within a story line (e.g., *The Letters Are Lost* by Lisa Campbell Ernst, *Kipper's A to Z: An Alphabet Adventure* by Mick Inkpen, or *What Pete Ate from A to Z* by Maira Kalman). In *The Letters Are Lost*, the letters (presented as a child's wooden blocks) become scattered and the story presents one letter at a time as each block is found. This book combines easy-to-read letters, along with a presentation of the sound of each letter (e.g., "C joined a family of Cows" and "D was a Dog's tasty toy") in a brightly illustrated, fun story. Another example that also incorporates a hunt for hidden letters is *Alphabetter* by Don Bar-el. In this story the characters need to find items that begin with a letter of the alphabet. Each page has the uppercase form of the letter and there is another letter hidden on each page, giving children an opportunity to actively hunt for the letter. As children become more skilled in visual identification of the letters of the alphabet there are many other books that will appeal to them. These titles present the letters in varied ways and shapes, such as *The Butterfly Alphabet* by Kjell Sandved, *Alphabet City* by Stephen T. Johnson, or *Z Goes Home* by Jon Agee. Not only are these books visually appealing, they also give children a chance to show off their letter knowledge by "finding" the letters in these complex pictures.

INTRODUCING LETTERS IN THE CHILD'S ENVIRONMENT

In addition to emphasizing alphabet knowledge through the use of books, it is also important to actively engage children in a variety of alphabet games and activities. Many of these activities are fairly simple and require few if any materials to set up. The activities can be easily paired with an alphabet book of your choice to reinforce the visual identification of letters.

Work with Children's Names and Other Important Letters

One simple way to introduce alphabet knowledge is by showing a child the first letter of her name and other important letters, such as her last name or sibling or pet names. This helps the child not only identify the letter, but connect it to something meaningful. By pointing out the letter ("Look, there's an *A* for Amanda"), we draw children's attention to the alphabet in their surroundings.

Alphabet Song (Sing-Along) and Tracking Activities with Visual Models

Another way to demonstrate the alphabet to young children is to recite the alphabet song. Repeating this song whenever you have the chance (e.g., when pushing your child on the swing or in the stroller, when preparing dinner, in the car, or during transitions between activities at day care) will reinforce the letters and help the child to remember them. In addition, you can point to images of letters as you sing along to the song. Your visual alphabet can be homemade or a store-bought version. Pairing the song with the letters will provide children with the knowledge of what each letter looks and sounds like, a crucial skill for emerging literacy.

Letter Hunts and Letter Naming

As children come to know their letters, a fun activity that can be done anywhere is letter hunts, where a child can find a given letter ("Can you find the *B*s in the room"?). Engaging children in active searching for the target letter in their environment supports the sound-letter connection and uses their new alphabet knowledge. Children can also point out and name their letters using books, foam models, magnetic letters, or other visuals of the alphabet. One particular book that encourages letter hunting in the environment is *Backseat A-B-See* by Maria van Lieshout, where road signs are presented as an example of each letter. This book could be used in the car with a child to encourage finding letters in the environment. Letter naming allows children to practice identifying the letters of the alphabet, preparing them to do so in the context of printed words as they learn to read.

Sorting Letters with Different Print Styles

When children become more familiar with the alphabet, sorting letters with different print styles provides them with an opportunity to look beyond specific differences in the way letters are formed to generalize the letter an image stands for. To support this understanding, caregivers, teachers, and librarians can create a simple letter sort. This letter sort can include images of different letters (cut from magazines or newspapers, handwritten, or printed) in a range of styles and fonts. Once the letters are mixed (one suggestion is to create card-size images of the letters by gluing them to sturdy pieces of cardboard and place them in a "mailbox" or "mailbag" that children can choose from), then children can place each letter in the proper pile, or in a labeled bag or box with the corresponding letter. This hands-on sorting activity requires active participation by the child.

Upper- and Lowercase Match

Once children become skilled at sorting across print styles, you can then introduce upper- and lowercase letters. Point out to children what lowercase and uppercase letters are, teaching them the correspondences between them (e.g., "This is an *A* and this is an *a*"). This activity can be done using many of the alphabet books that were discussed earlier. By having a child match up the upper- and lowercase letter pairs (possibly as part of a letter sort like the type that was described above), children are learning to recognize and identify letters in various forms in text.

Letter Formation in Air, in Sand, on Carpet, with Clay, or with Other Manipulatives

To engage all of children's senses, letter formation in air (for example, "drawing" the letter with your finger), in sand, on carpet, with paint, pasta, beads, blocks, or clay (or other manipulatives) will help children to "feel" the alphabet and remind them of their shapes and how they sound. Dry-erase boards with a variety of colorful markers also provide another opportunity for children to practice writing letters. You could start out by providing the child with a model to trace and then have the child practice writing the letters on his or her own. Sidewalk chalk used on any paved surface is a good way to get children to practice their letters while enjoying some time outside. Another fun activity is to have children use their bodies to make the shapes of letters. Not only does this continue to reinforce alphabet knowledge, it also makes learning fun and active. Young children learn best when multiple "modes" of learning are employed.

ALPHABET KNOWLEDGE ACTIVITY IDEAS: SUMMARY

(activities appropriate for younger children are listed first)

Work with children's names and other important letters
Alphabet song (sing-along) and tracking activities with visual models
Letter hunts and letter naming
Sorting letters with different print styles
Upper- and lowercase match
Letter formation in air, in sand, on carpet, with clay, or with other manipulatives

ALPHABET KNOWLEDGE GOALS

The activities described above are designed to elicit a working knowledge of the alphabet—of the sound and look of individual letters, of which letters appear in important words (such as a child's name), and that letters have both upper- and lowercase versions. In addition, we provided several examples of children's books good for demonstrating this alphabet knowledge. To help guide you to assess whether this knowledge has been applied, we provide a list (ordered from activities appropriate for younger to older children) of alphabet knowledge goals below for your emerging reader. Remember that these are just suggested goals and many children will not accomplish all of these milestones until the end of kindergarten. Children do not need to know how to say all of the sounds, nor do they need to know how to form letters before kindergarten, but the ability to recognize twenty letters will give children a good head start.

ALPHABET KNOWLEDGE GOALS: SUMMARY

Identify twenty uppercase letters
Identify twelve lowercase letters
Know sound for four to twelve letters
Recite the alphabet song, while pointing to letters
Write down letter for two to three sounds
Write own name

ALPHABET KNOWLEDGE RISK

The goals listed above are guidelines to help you estimate how your child is progressing. Remember that there is a wide range in children's development, and not all children will reach these goals easily. Many children who are just learning the alphabet will confuse letters and numbers. This is not a concern early on, as letters and numbers don't yet have a function. However, a child who does not recognize the first letter in his or her name may not have had adequate exposure to print, and this could be cause for some concern. If this difficulty persists even after the alphabet has been taught and the child has had lots of opportunities to become familiar with them, then that child may need some extra attention.

RECOMMENDED BOOKS FOR ALPHABET KNOWLEDGE

Z Goes Home	Jon Agee
Alphabetter	Don Bar-el
Alligator Alphabet	Stella Blackstone and Stephanie Bauer
Eric Carle's ABC	Eric Carle
The Letters Are Lost	Lisa Campbell Ernst
Kipper's A to Z: An Alphabet Adventure	Mick Inkpen
Alphabet City	Stephen T. Johnson
What Pete Ate from A to Z	Maira Kalman
Alphabatics	Suse MacDonald

Chicka Chicka Boom Boom	Bill Martin Jr., John Archambault, and Lois Ehlert
Flora McDonnell's ABC	Flora McDonnell
The Butterfly Alphabet	Kjell Sandved
Richard Scarry's Find Your ABC's	Richard Scarry
Dr. Seuss's ABC: An Amazing Alphabet Book	Dr. Seuss (Theodor Geisel)
Backseat A-B-See	Maria van Lieshout
ABeCedarios (English and Spanish)	Cynthia Weill

HOW-TO ACTIVITY: We're Going on a Letter Hunt!

When a child becomes newly familiar with a letter or letters, you could spend a day choosing and searching for that letter (for example, *M* on Mondays, or *T* on Tuesdays). As you move about that day, running errands, dropping off at preschool, or as part of the day-care curriculum you could make a game of finding the chosen letter. For example, you could point out to your child, "Look, there is a *J* on that bottle of juice."

As part of the game, you could give points or rewards (perhaps a treat) for each letter found, or you could photograph the most interesting examples of the letter that you find in the community to print and hang up on a "wall of fame" for your chosen letter.

When you return home, you can extend the letter hunt to books or other items in your home. Your child could look through the pantry or a book or magazine for evidence of your chosen letter.

In addition, you could use household items to create your letter. For lunch or dinner, you could create your letter out of pasta, bread, or veggies. Or, for a special dessert or at snack time, you could bake cookies in your letter shape.

HOW-TO ACTIVITY: Name Sort

This activity works well with a group of children at a library story hour, preschool, or day-care setting. Write each child's name on a sturdy piece of cardboard. After working with children to identify the names and the first letter of each name, you can have the children sort the names in alphabetical order. Providing them with a clear example of the alphabet for them to match to would be helpful here.

Word Sort

A similar activity (that could work at home as well as in a group setting) would be to have children sort familiar words into alphabetical order. Start by making cards with names of fruits or vegetables, family members, animals, or any other groups of words that your child finds interesting. After helping the children to read each word, you could then let them sort the words alphabetically.

REFERENCES

Adams, Marilyn Jager. *Beginning to Read: Thinking and Learning about Print.* Cambridge, Mass.: MIT Press paperback edition, 1994.

Scarborough, Hollis. "Early Identification of Children at Risk for Reading Disabilities: Phonological Awareness and Some Other Promising Predictors." In *Specific Reading Disability: A View of the Spectrum*, edited by Bruce K. Shapiro, Pasquale J. Accardo, and Arnold J. Capute, 75–119. Timonium, Md.: York, 1998.

BIBLIOGRAPHY

Agee, Jon. *Z Goes Home.* Illus. by the author. New York: Hyperion, 2003. 32 p.

Bar-el, Don. *Alphabetter.* Illus. by Graham Ross. Custer, Wash.: Orca, 2007. 32 p.

Blackstone, Stella. *Alligator Alphabet.* Illus. by Stephanie Bauer. Cambridge, Mass.: Barefoot, 2005. 32 p.

Carle, Eric. *Eric Carle's ABC.* Illus. by the author. New York: Penguin, 2007. 16 p.

Ernst, Lisa Campbell. *The Letters Are Lost.* Illus. by the author. New York: Viking, 1996. 32 p.

Inkpen, Mick. *Kipper's A to Z: An Alphabet Adventure.* Illus. by the author. San Diego, Calif.: Harcourt, 2000. 64 p.

Johnson, Stephen T. *Alphabet City.* Illus. by the author. New York: Puffin, 1995. 32 p.

Kalman, Maira. *What Pete Ate from A to Z.* Illus. by the author. New York: Putnam, 2001. 48 p.

MacDonald, Suse. *Alphabatics.* Illus. by the author. New York: Aladdin, 1992. 64 p.

Martin, Bill, and John Archambault. *Chicka Chicka Boom Boom.* Illus. by Lois Ehlert. New York: Simon & Schuster, 1989. 36 p.

McDonnell, Flora. *Flora McDonnell's ABC.* Illus. by the author. Cambridge, Mass.: Candlewick, 1997. 36 p.

Sandved, Kjell. *The Butterfly Alphabet.* Illus. by the author. New York: Scholastic, 1996. 64 p.

Scarry, Richard. *Richard Scarry's Find Your ABC's.* New York: Sterling, 2009. 32 p.

Seuss, Dr. *Dr. Seuss's ABC.* Illus. by the author. New York: Random House, 1963. 32 p.

van Lieshout, Maria. *Backseat A-B-See.* Illus. by the author. San Francisco: Chronicle, 2012. 40 p.

Weill, Cynthia. *ABeCedarios: Mexican Folk Art ABCs in English and Spanish.* Illus. by Moises Jimenez and Armando Jimenez. El Paso, Tex.: Cinco Puntos, 2007. 32 p.

4

BOOK-HANDLING SKILLS AND CONCEPTS ABOUT PRINT

Fill your house with stacks of books, in all the crannies and all the nooks.

—Dr. Seuss

In this chapter we discuss the crucial role of experience with books in setting the stage for the emergent reader. "Knowing" about books includes knowing the difference between the words and the pictures, the front and back of the book, and tracking print from left to right. A child who does not know how to hold a book—who does not recognize front from back, top from bottom, has probably had very limited exposure to books. Again, research shows that this knowledge is an important precursor for later reading success. While it is not difficult to teach most children these basic skills, a child who lacks these *book-handling skills* is likely to be unfamiliar with many components of how books are organized. Further, even young children who have been read to at home often don't know the differences between the role of the words on the pages and the pictures. Specifically, young children may not understand that a reader is reading the words and not simply telling the story by describing the pictures. It is up to you to teach them. These *concepts about print* can be rapidly taught through shared book reading. However, as with alphabet knowledge, book-handling skills and concepts about print are not sufficient to make a child a reader, but part of the necessary building blocks for later reading development. Finally, in this chapter we also introduce the idea of *speech-to-print matching*, where children are able to understand that a given spoken word in a book has a related printed form.

BOOK-HANDLING SKILLS

How to Handle a Book

Note that basic book-handling skills are for children with little book experience, so begin with very simple books. Even infants enjoy being read to, and there are many board books and soft books of this type that are easy for very young children to hold and explore. Infants may turn pages, bang or shake books, or even explore books by mouthing them. Giving children access to books as early as possible will introduce them to book handling and familiarize them with the purpose of books. A number of popular authors have books in board book form, including Dr. Seuss (e.g., *Dr. Seuss's ABC, Mr. Brown Can Moo, Can You?, Cat in the Hat, and One Fish, Two Fish*), Sandra Boynton (e.g., *Blue Hat, Green Hat, Doggies, Moo, Baa, La La La, and Hippos Go Berserk*), Eric Carle (e.g., *The Very Hungry Caterpillar, My Very First Book of Colors, The Very Lonely Firefly*), and other classics, such as *Goodnight Moon* and *The Runaway Bunny* by Margaret Wise Brown and Clement Hurd and *Big Red Barn* by Margaret Wise Brown and Felicia Bond. Allowing even a very young child or infant to hold books and turn pages promotes book-handling skills.

An example of a very simple book to start with for toddlers or preschoolers is a book like *I Went Walking* by Sue Williams, which has a repeated refrain ("I went walking." "What did you see?") and can be read again and again. One pattern children might like is to have you say, "I went walking," and they can respond, "What did you see?" Then they can answer "I saw a ____ looking at me." After you demonstrate this, you can allow the child to hold the book, turn the pages, and take turns with you using the repeated refrain. A similar title is *Brown Bear, Brown Bear, What Do You See?* by Bill Martin Jr. Simple books with repeated refrains allow children to come to know the story and actively engage with what is happening in the book.

Recognize That It Is Print and Not Pictures That Is Read in Stories

The next step beyond introducing to children how to enjoy and manipulate books is to teach them that it is print, and not pictures, that is read in stories. Because many children's books have colorful illustrations to catch children's attention and to support and enhance the story, it may not be clear to the child that what is being read from the book is *words* (or print). This *concept of print* refers to the ability to understand that it is the words on the page that are important in telling the story. As children develop, you can work toward a *speech-to-print match*, which means being able to point to separate printed words for a well-memorized chant. Books that work well to introduce concepts about print include books with large, clear font and repetitive, rhythmic books with few words per page. Children first learn to chant the refrain and then match spoken with written words. Some examples of this are the refrains "Jump, frog, jump!" in the book by the same name by Robert Kalan or "Cows in the pasture, moo, moo, moo" in *Barnyard Banter* by Denise Fleming. The chant in the book *Jump, Frog, Jump!*, which appears on every other page, becomes quickly memorized when frog has to jump to escape hungry fish and snakes. In *Barnyard Banter* there are a number of words that are repeated in the story, such as "Cows in the pasture, moo, moo, moo" or "Hens in the henhouse, cluck, cluck, cluck." In books that have a repeated refrain, you can use both picture and pattern so that the child can anticipate the next line. You can easily follow along with your finger as you read the book to point out the word that is being said (e.g., "Moo, moo, moo"). If you are working with a large group of children, a book with large print could be propped on an easel and a pointer could be used to point to each of the words. By doing this, you teach the emerging reader that the words that you are identifying stand for the word that he or she is hearing. A great example of a book that would work well with a large group of children is *Rain* by Manya Stojic. It is a simple story of the animals of the savanna using their senses to track a coming rainstorm. While this might not be a story children could participate in, the words are printed in bold, large print and will easily capture their attention. It is important to remember that as we introduce these principles to children we need to be as explicit as possible. As skilled readers we take for granted that it is print that is read, and we go horizontally from left to right, but children often need to be taught these seemingly simple concepts.

Differentiate between Letters, Numbers, Words, and Pictures

When children come to understand the relationship of *speech to print* the next step is to educate children to differentiate between letters, numbers, words, and pictures in a book. Once children recognize that it is print (and not pictures) that is read in stories, you can point out which symbols are letters, words, numbers, and pictures. Examples of books that incorporate both letters and numbers for younger children are *Counting Kisses* by Karen Katz, *Five Little Monkeys Play Hide-and-Seek* by Eileen Christelow, *My First Counting Book* by Lilian Moore, and *One Boy* by Laura Vaccaro Seeger. For slightly older children, *The Water Hole* by Graeme Base presents both letters and numbers with a story appropriate for preschoolers and early school-age children. This step will pair nicely with alphabet knowledge discussed in the previous chapter. Many of the alphabet books can also be used to encourage book-handling skills and concepts about print.

BOOK HANDLING AND CONCEPTS ABOUT PRINT GOALS

(goals appropriate for younger children are listed first)

Hold a book and turn pages appropriately
Work *toward* speech-to-print match by:

Recognizing that it is print (and not pictures) that is read in stories
Differentiating between letters, numbers, words, and pictures

BOOK HANDLING AND CONCEPTS ABOUT PRINT RISK

A child who does not know how to hold a book, who does not recognize front from back, top from bottom, will likely have had limited or no exposure to books. As we have discussed in this chapter, it is not difficult to teach most children these basic skills. However, if you are a librarian or day-care provider you may find that a child who lacks these book-handling skills is likely to be unfamiliar with other components of story time (listening to stories, talking about stories, etc.). It may be helpful to give this child, and perhaps his or her family, personal attention in order for the child to receive maximum benefit from story time. If you are a librarian, you could invite the parents to listen in during story time. As a day-care provider you could invite a parent to come in and share a book with the children, or send the child home with a special book to share with the family.

RECOMMENDED BOOKS FOR BOOK-HANDLING SKILLS AND CONCEPTS ABOUT PRINT

The Water Hole	Graeme Base
Blue Hat, Green Hat	Sandra Boynton
Doggies	Sandra Boynton
Hippos Go Berserk	Sandra Boynton
Moo, Baa, La La La	Sandra Boynton
Big Red Barn	Margaret Wise Brown

Goodnight Moon	Margaret Wise Brown
The Runaway Bunny	Margaret Wise Brown
My Very First Book of Colors	Eric Carle
The Very Hungry Caterpillar	Eric Carle
The Very Lonely Firefly	Eric Carle
Jesse Bear, What Will You Wear?	Nancy White Carlstrom
Five Little Monkeys Play Hide-and-Seek	Eileen Christelow
Barnyard Banter	Denise Fleming
Is Your Mama a Llama?	Deborah Guarino
Jump, Frog, Jump!	Robert Kalan
Counting Kisses	Karen Katz
Brown Bear, Brown Bear, What Do You See?	Bill Martin Jr.
My First Counting Book	Lilian Moore
We're Going on a Bear Hunt	Michael Rosen and Helen Oxenbury
One Boy	Laura Vaccaro Seeger
The Cat in the Hat	Dr. Seuss
Dr. Seuss's ABC	Dr. Seuss
Mr. Brown Can Moo, Can You?	Dr. Seuss
One Fish, Two Fish, Red Fish, Blue Fish	Dr. Seuss
Rain	Manya Stojic
I Went Walking	Sue Williams
Bear Snores On	Karma Wilson

HOW-TO ACTIVITY: Book Handling

(appropriate for younger children, approximately two to four years, with any familiar board book)

The goal of book handling is to encourage young children to be comfortable with the purpose of a book and how to "read" it appropriately. For this activity any book that a child loves will work well, although board books are sturdier for younger children to manipulate.

Using the child's chosen book, you can encourage him or her to "read" it to an audience. The audience could be a group of children at a day care, siblings at home, or even the child's stuffed animals or dolls. Help the child to set up by creating a cozy spot to sit with the intended audience. If you are at a day care or preschool, you could allow the child to sit in the teacher's chair to read the book. At home, you could use a special chair and arrange the audience around the child on the floor.

Encourage the child to "read" the book to the audience (which may just mean having the child tell the familiar story as he or she remembers it). Help the child to hold the book in the proper orientation and show the pictures to his or her audience.

HOW-TO ACTIVITY: Concepts about Print

Using the Book The Very Hungry Caterpillar *by Eric Carle*
Create a category sort for letters, numbers, words, and pictures. In order to explicitly teach children to differentiate letters, numbers, words, and pictures, choose a favorite book that the child is very familiar with and that has simple words and images.

Using *The Very Hungry Caterpillar* as a model, you and your child could visit Eric-Carle.com and find downloadable printable coloring pages from the book. After coloring the pictures of the caterpillar and the food he eats, you can copy down letters (or help the child copy them), numbers (perhaps the number of foods the caterpillar eats, such as 2 pears, 3 plums, or 4 strawberries), and simple words that appear in the book. If you do not have access to the printables, you can draw the images yourself.

Once you have your letters, words, pictures, and numbers, cut each out to a single sheet and place in a box or bag. Let the child pick an item out and tell you whether it is a word, a letter, a picture, or a number, and what it is. Once the child identifies the item, you can place it in a pile or a box for that category so that all the words go together, the numbers, and so forth.

BIBLIOGRAPHY

Base, Graeme. *The Water Hole*. Illus. by the author. New York: Abrams, 2001. 32 p.

Boynton, Sandra. *Blue Hat, Green Hat*. Illus. by the author. New York: Simon & Schuster, 1984. 14 p.

——. *Doggies*. Illus. by the author. New York: Simon & Schuster, 1984. 14 p.

——. *Hippos Go Berserk*. New York: Simon & Schuster, 1977. 16 p.

——. *Moo, Baa, La La La*. Illus. by the author. New York: Simon & Schuster, 1982. 14 p.

Brown, Margaret Wise. *Big Red Barn*. Illus. by Felicia Bond. New York: Harper-Collins, 1956. 32 p.

——. *Goodnight Moon*. Illus. by Clement Hurd. New York: HarperCollins, 1947. 30 p.

——. *The Runaway Bunny*. Illus. by Clement Hurd. New York: HarperCollins, 1942. 48 p.

Carle, Eric. *My Very First Book of Colors*. Illus. by the author. New York: Philomel, 1974. 20 p.

——. *The Very Hungry Caterpillar*. Illus. by the author. New York: Philomel, 1969. 13 p.

——. *The Very Lonely Firefly*. Illus. by the author. New York: Philomel, 1995. 14 p.

Carlstrom, Nancy White. *Jesse Bear, What Will You Wear?* Illus. by Bruce Degen. New York: Simon & Schuster, 1986. 32 p.

Christelow, Eileen. *Five Little Monkeys Play Hide-and-Seek*. Illus. by the author. New York: Houghton Mifflin, 2004. 40 p.

Fleming, Denise. *Barnyard Banter*. Illus. by the author. New York: Holt, 1994. 32 p.

Guarino, Deborah. *Is Your Mama a Llama?* Illus. by Steven Kellogg. New York: Scholastic, 1989. 32 p.

Kalan, Robert. *Jump, Frog, Jump!* Illus. by Byron Barton. New York: Greenwillow, 1981. 32 p.

Katz, Karen. *Counting Kisses*. Illus. by the author. New York: Simon & Schuster, 2001. 32 p.

Martin, Bill. *Brown Bear, Brown Bear, What Do You See?* Illus. by Eric Carle. New York: Holt, 1992. 32 p.

Moore, Lilian. *My First Counting Book*. Illus. by Garth Williams. New York: Random House, 1956. 24 p.

Rosen, Michael. *We're Going on a Bear Hunt*. Illus. by Helen Oxenbury. New York: Simon & Schuster, 1989. 36 p.

Seeger, Laura Vaccaro. *One Boy*. Illus. by the author. New York: Roaring Brook, 2008. 48 p.

Seuss, Dr. *The Cat in the Hat*. Illus. by the author. New York: Random House, 1957. 61 p.

——. *Dr. Seuss's ABC*. Illus. by the author. New York: Random House, 1963. 32 p.

——. *Mr. Brown Can Moo, Can You?* Illus. by the author. New York: Random House, 1970. 36 p.

——. *One Fish, Two Fish, Red Fish, Blue Fish.* Illus. by the author. New York: Random House, 1960. 63 p.

Stojic, Manya. *Rain.* Illus. by the author. New York: Crown, 2000. 32 p.

Williams, Sue. *I Went Walking.* Illus. by Julie Vivas. San Diego, Calif.: Harcourt, 1990. 32 p.

Wilson, Karma. *Bear Snores On.* Illus. by Jane Chapman. New York: Simon & Schuster, 2001. 34 p.

PHONOLOGICAL AWARENESS

To learn to read is to light a fire; every syllable that is spelled out is a spark.

—Victor Hugo

Phonological awareness is one of the single most important skills that children need to acquire as a foundation for learning to read. This chapter will focus on the significance of phonological awareness in reading development. Before beginning to discuss the books and activities that will help to promote this important precursor, we need to first clarify what phonological awareness is and how it contributes to early reading success.

WHAT IS PHONOLOGICAL AWARENESS?

The term *phonological* refers to the sound structure of speech. All spoken words are made up of sounds, called *phonemes*. Phonemes are the basic units of speech. Changing one phoneme in a word can change the meaning of a word. For example, the word *bit* is made up of three separate phonemes, /b/ /i/ /t/. If you change the /i/ to /a/ you get the word *bat*. Most typically developing young children can easily learn to recognize and produce the phonemes of their native language; however, most children (and even some adults) are not consciously aware of these speech sounds. Most of us would have difficulty identifying individual speech sounds in words even though we routinely produce these sounds!

Phonological awareness is a general term that refers to the understanding that spoken words are made up of combinations of recurring sounds. For example, phonological awareness is necessary to understand that "cat" and "car" have something in common (that they start with the same sound) or that "cat" and "bat" rhyme (that they share the same ending sounds).

Phonological awareness can be broken down into two components, *phonological sensitivity* and *phonemic awareness*. *Phonological sensitivity* allows children to notice similarities in the sounds of words at a more global level. This includes word length ("butterfly" is longer than "pot"), number of syllables ("dog" has one syllable, "dinosaur" has three), and shared rhymes ("box" and "fox" rhyme). The growth of phonological sensitivity contributes to the development of *phonemic awareness,* which is a more fine-grained analysis that includes the understanding that spoken words are composed of a series of individual consonants and vowels sounds, or phonemes. Phonemic awareness is demonstrated by the ability to segment words into these components (say all the sounds in "glass") or identify the common parts across words (e.g., the first sound in "stop" is the final sound in "pots"). Phonemic awareness is not an all-or-none skill, but rather one that continues to develop, often in tandem with early literacy, until age seven and beyond. Even for individuals who are sensitive to the sounds of words (young children love to rhyme!), the ability to identify individual speech sounds is very difficult. Thus, phonemic awareness almost always requires explicit instruction as a child is learning to read. At this point, it is necessary to clarify that having an awareness of the sounds of language (and the ability to manipulate these sounds) does not mean that a child is reading. However, phonemic awareness is a crucial step in the development of reading because it enables children to understand the *alphabetic principle*. The *alphabetic principle* is the idea that we use letters and letter patterns to represent the sounds of spoken language. Learning the relationships between letters and their sounds is the key to cracking the reading code. This is what enables children to sound out both familiar and unfamiliar words in print. To see the importance of developing the ability to decode print, consider the child who does not acquire it. This child would be forced to memorize the overall shapes of huge numbers of words without any appreciation of the systematic spelling-sound correspondences. Thus, well beyond kindergarten and first grade the awareness of phonemes will continue to distinguish more skilled readers from less skilled ones (Liberman, Shankweiler, Camp, Blachman, and Werfelman, 1980; Shankweiler and Fowler, 2004).

WHY IS PHONOLOGICAL AWARENESS NECESSARY?

Many studies have supported the importance of phonological awareness in learning to read. For example, research has shown that children who have some phonological awareness before learning to read (at ages four and five) show better reading skills in later grades (Bradley and Bryant, 1983). Importantly, other studies have shown that training in phonological awareness before learning to read also results in better reading skills in later grades (Bradley and Bryant, 1985). While the more complex aspects of phonemic awareness will likely be beyond the capacity of a preschool-aged child, there are many things that can be done to encourage the development of the awareness of the sounds of language and the ability to manipulate them.

In fact, research has shown that young children who have more exposure to simple nursery rhymes, to letters, and to reading activities have better awareness of phonemes later on (Bryant, MacLean, Bradley, and Crossland, 1990; Whitehurst and Lonigan, 1998).

In the following sections, we outline books and activities that will support the development of various phonological awareness skills. While the eventual goal is to build full phonemic awareness, many preschool-aged children are not yet ready for this, thus we will focus mainly on development of phonological sensitivity.

GENERAL PRINCIPLES FOR INTRODUCING PHONOLOGICAL AWARENESS

In introducing phonological awareness, some guidelines based on research can be applied. As discussed in the first chapter, it is important to be explicit about what you want the child to learn, so planning in advance is vital. With phonological skills, it is also crucial that skills are introduced in a developmentally appropriate way. We know that phonological sensitivity precedes phonemic awareness, so we need to introduce these skills first. Before decomposing words into their phonemes, books and activities should be focused on detecting similarities of larger sound units including rhyme (such as c<u>at</u> and m<u>at</u>) and onsets, the beginning part of words before the vowel (such as <u>sh</u>ip and <u>sh</u>ell). When drawing children's attention to sound properties of words, focus on a few well-selected phonemes and phoneme combinations. (Later in this chapter we will help you to select sounds that are easiest for children to identify and we will guide you to books and activities that will incorporate these sounds.) In keeping with the importance of practice and engaging multiple modes, children should not be just passively listening to sounds, but also reproducing them as well. For example, books with lots of repetition with a specific sound (such as Kevin Henkes's *Wemberly Worried*, which includes repeated use of the /w/ sound with text like "Wemberly worried"; "'You worry too much,' said her mother. 'When you worry, I worry,' said her father. 'Worry, worry, worry,' said her grandmother") will allow you to point out the sound and have the child repeat it (for example, by taking the role of the grandmother and saying her "lines"). This gives children an active role and allows them to say and practice the sound or sounds that you have been working with. The key to all the skills and activities introduced in this chapter, and the other chapters in this book, is that these are simple and fun activities that can have large payoffs later on for your child!

INTRODUCTION TO PHONOLOGICAL AWARENESS

One fun way to begin to get young children interested in the sounds of language is to introduce them to books that emphasize the sounds of words in an appealing way. For example, *Rattletrap Car* by Phyllis Root includes such phrases as "Clinked clanked bing bang pop!," *Slop Goes the Soup* by Pamela Duncan Edwards includes the words "pop chop slam bubble bumpity-bump crunch," or *Squeak, Rumble, Whomp! Whomp! Whomp!* by Wynton Marsalis, which has words like "grumble, rumble" and "squeaks, speaks." *Violet's Music* by Angela Johnson and *Roar and More* by Karla Kuskin also encourage children to engage in the sounds around them. There are also many wonderful books of children's poetry that will encourage attention to the sounds of words. A few suggestions are *Chinese Mother Goose Rhymes* by Robert Wyndham, *Sing a Song of Popcorn* by Beatrice Schenk de Regniers et al., eds., and *Falling Up* by Shel Silverstein. All of these books are fun both to read and to listen to and they highlight the sounds of words.

PHONOLOGICAL SENSITIVITY

As children first begin to learn how to read, their overall phonological awareness is developed through phonological sensitivity. Again, phonological sensitivity is the ability to recognize specific attributes of units of words that are larger than phonemes. One important concept involved in phonological sensitivity is the production and recognition of rhyming words. Children as young as two years of age are sensitive to words that rhyme (Lonigan, Burgess, Anthony, and Barker, 1998). The ability to recognize and produce rhyming words is central to the overall development of phonological awareness. Examples of simple books that introduce children to rhyming are *There's a Wocket in My Pocket* by Dr. Seuss, *Is Your Mama a Llama?* by Deborah Guarino, *Fox in Socks* by Dr. Seuss, *Sheep in a Jeep* by Nancy Shaw, *One Fish, Two Fish, Red Fish, Blue Fish* by Dr. Seuss, and *Jamberry* by Bruce Degen. For children who are learning more than one language, introducing rhymes in either language will be useful. There are several good books that present rhyming words in Spanish, for example. These include *Bebe Goes Shopping*, *Say Hola to Spanish*, and *Say Hola to Spanish at the Circus*, all by Susan Middleton Elya. In addition to simple rhyming there are a number of properties of words that are essential to the development of phonological awareness in emergent readers. Next, we further explore these properties and recommend additional books and activities for each one.

SYLLABLES

A key element in developing phonological sensitivity is the ability to recognize syllables in words. Syllables are bigger units than phonemes (and bigger than onsets or rhymes) and are the larger building blocks of a word. For example, the word *water* can be broken down into two syllables ("wa" and "ter") while *butterfly* contains three syllables ("bu" "ter" "fly"). Teaching children to recognize syllables can be done with some simple activities and through the use of books. One such activity can be done by asking children to "clap out" words into syllables. A nice way to introduce this skill is by incorporating a child's name. You can first demonstrate how to clap out the syllables in your name and then work with the child to clap the syllables in her own name (e.g., Meredith, "Mer" clap, "e," clap, "dith" clap). After children become familiar with this activity, it can be expanded to include vocabulary words from favorite stories or poems (e.g., clap for each syllable in the word *elephant*, "el" "e" "phant"). Any engaging book that your child enjoys could be incorporated into this activity—particularly books that use words of varying length. For example, for a child who is interested in dinosaurs, *Dinosaur A–Z* by Roger Priddy would be a wonderful book to demonstrate syllables (for example, "Fab" "ro" "saur" "us").

Another activity that helps children develop phonological sensitivity is syllable deletion. After working with a child to count syllables in words, you could then show how words are composed by pointing out segments within words. For example, you can ask a child, "Say the word *cowboy*. Now say cowboy without the *boy*" or "Say butterfly. Now say butterfly without saying *fly*." This attention to the separate syllables of the words will further encourage phonological sensitivity. This is a fun and simple activity that can easily be done anywhere!

For children who have mastered counting syllables and syllable deletion, you could then move on to counting and categorizing words by number of syllables. The book *Tops & Bottoms* by Janet Stevens illustrates vegetables that grow aboveground (the tops) and belowground (the bottoms). After reading the story together and discussing the various vegetables (which might also include introducing some new vocabulary words, discussed further in chapter 6), you could label the vegetables and sort them by the number of syllables. You could use plastic vegetables or pictures on a flannel board (a large piece of flannel glued to cardboard with objects cut out of flannel that will stick to the larger piece) to first identify the vegetables and determine which grow aboveground (lettuce, broccoli, or celery) and compare them to those that grow belowground (radish, carrots, or beets). For syllable counting, you could then choose different vegetables, count out their syllables, and then group them by which have one, two, or three syllables. For example, those that have one syllable, like corn or beets, those with two syllables, such as radish, lettuce, and carrot, and those that have three syllables, like broccoli and celery. Again, you can tailor this activity to the particular interests of the child. For example, dinosaur words would be wonderful to sort by the number of syllables. The point of working on these syllable skills is for the child to begin to have an awareness of the sounds of the spoken language and the ability to manipulate these sounds.

SYLLABLE SEGMENTING ACTIVITY IDEAS: SUMMARY

(activities appropriate for younger children are listed first)

Clap out syllables in child's name or words from favorite poems or books
Segment familiar words or words from books
Delete syllables
Count and categorize words by number of syllables

RHYME PRODUCTION AND RECOGNITION

As mentioned earlier, attention to rhyme is another important component of phonological sensitivity. Two words rhyme when they are identical from the stressed syllable to the end of the word, such as bl<u>ack</u> s<u>ack</u> and ban<u>ana</u> cab<u>ana</u>. In addition to introducing rhyming through books (as mentioned earlier in this chapter) there are many other activities that help to encourage both recognition of rhyming words and production of rhymes. A great place to start to familiarize children with rhyme is nursery rhymes and chants that incorporate rhyme (e.g., "Rain, rain go aw<u>ay</u>, come again another d<u>ay</u>" or "Twinkle, twinkle little st<u>ar</u>, how I wonder what you <u>are</u>"). Once you introduce rhyme, you can query children directly, asking them, "Does this rhyme?" (Cat/Hat, Box/Lip?). You can also ask them to come up with their own rhymes: "What rhymes with back, rack . . . ?" Children can repeat and even add to rhyming pairs using books like *Bear Snores On* by Karma Wilson and *Sheep in a Jeep* by Nancy Shaw. These rhyming books can involve active participation by children, for example, by using the images from the book to have the child repeat phrases, such as "Sheep shout, Jeep comes out" (from *Sheep in a Jeep* by Nancy Shaw). Or have them produce the rhyme by anticipating what comes next. You read, "Sheep yelp. Sheep get . . . ?," pausing for the child to fill in the missing rhyming word ("help").

To assist children in recognizing rhyme, a good activity is to sort cards picturing rhyming words from books. These cards are easily constructed using cardboard and pictures cut from magazines or downloaded from Internet image searches. For example, children could sort images of /eep/ words (sheep, jeep, from *Sheep in a Jeep* by Nancy Shaw) and /oks/ words (fox, socks, from *Fox in Socks* by Dr. Seuss). Another fun activity is to play "Sound-tration" (like the memory game Concentration) with rhyming pairs. For this activity, you could use cards with pictures of rhyming words developed for the sorting task (/eep/ words and /oks/ words) and add some other rhyming words from another book (e.g., *Bear Snores On* by Karma Wilson). The cards would all be spread out facedown and the first player would turn over two cards. If the two cards rhyme, the child would pick up the cards and take another turn; if not, the cards would be turned facedown again and the next player would take a turn. The game incorporates both a memory piece and the recognition of rhyming words.

The ability to *produce* rhymes is another important component of phonological awareness. Production requires that the child say the rhyme and encourages active participation. To encourage production you could use a simple rhyming cube activity. You can create a rhyming cube with six pictures from a book you have read with the children. Secure the pictures to six sides of a cube with clear packing tape. Have the children take turns "rolling" the cube. Each child then has to come up with a word that rhymes with that picture. When creating your rhyming cube, make sure to use simple one- or two-syllable words that the children recognize.

As with other skills introduced so far, it is important to engage children on multiple levels and to keep it fun. You don't need to spend a lot of time on each activity and can also encourage movement with the songs and chants that you introduce. Incorporate books that you and your child enjoy that focus on rhyming. In addition to the simple rhyming books identified earlier in this chapter, other notable rhyming books include *Hush! A Thai Lullaby* by Minfong Ho, *Charlie Parker Played Be Bop* by Chris Raschka, *This Jazz Man* by Karen Ehrhardt, and *I Like Myself* by Karen Beaumont. All present rhyme in a lyrical, musical fashion and are great fun to read and listen to.

RHYMING ACTIVITY IDEAS: SUMMARY

(activities appropriate for younger children are listed first)

Choose simple rhyming books
Anticipate the story line on the basis of rhyme, picture
Repeat (and add to) rhyming pairs
Recognize rhyming words by identifying words from books that rhyme
Play "Sound-tration" with rhyming pairs
Produce rhymes using a rhyming cube

ALLITERATION

An additional skill that contributes to phonological awareness is alliteration. Alliteration is the ability to recognize the repetition of the same sounds at the beginning of words known as word onsets (initial sound before the first vowel). An example of alliteration is the /l/ sound in "Lawrence the leopard made lemonade." In preschool and kindergarten, the ability to match words on the basis of beginning sounds is an excellent predictor of reading success. However, most children need explicit guidance in attending to the initial phonemes or sounds of words, and for most children the ability to rhyme comes before the ability to notice alliteration. Like the rhyming and syllable tasks, it is important to introduce alliteration in stages to meet the child's abilities. The easiest first step is to isolate the word onset by asking children to say the beginning of a word or to "say just a little bit of show [/sh/] or my [/m/]." When working on isolating beginning sounds, certain sounds that can be prolonged are easier to begin with such as /m/, /n/, /z/, /f/, /v/, /s/, /sh/ and vowel sounds such as /a/, /i/, /u/, /o/ before other sounds such as /p/, /t/, /k/, /b/, /d/, and /g/. Books that focus on one or two initial sounds are best to begin with to help foster this skill during story time. In *Some Smug Slug* by Pamela Duncan Edwards, the focus is on the initial /s/ sound as in "One summer Sunday while strolling on soil." Other good examples are *Wemberly Worried* by Kevin Henkes and *"Slowly, Slowly, Slowly," Said the Sloth* by Eric Carle. Once children are able to isolate some of those first sounds you can move to books that incorporate other sounds. Some good examples of books are *Dr. Seuss's ABC* (which includes multiple examples for each sound), *Pigs in Pajamas* by Maggie Smith, and *Many Marvelous Monsters* by Ed Heck. When working on alliteration it is important for the child to practice isolating the sounds by having him or her produce the sounds. When reading books with the child, you could have the child repeat back some of the key phrases in the book that emphasize the initial sound. The goal for alliteration is for the child to be able to identify the initial sound, that is, to recognize that "pan" and "pink" start the same. Learning to identify the first sound sets the stage for the child to later learn to segment an entire word into all of its phonemes (e.g., to know that "pan" is made up of /p/, /a/, /n/).

Many of the activities that were used to promote rhyming skill can be adapted for alliteration. Instead of matching pictures of words that rhyme in Sound-tration, you could have children match picture cards depicting the same initial sound. You could also adapt the rhyming cube to focus on initial sounds instead, which incorporates a production aspect into the activity. Another activity, similar to one used to promote alphabet knowledge, is to have children sort objects and pictures with the same initial sound into labeled "mailbags" or boxes. Plastic food and small toys would work very well with this activity. You can also combine the alliteration activities with alphabet knowledge, by having the children connect the target phoneme(s) with letter(s) by using plastic letters, air, carpet or sand writing, or writing on paper.

The goal of these alliteration activities is to begin to foster a secure awareness of the sounds of language. Keep in mind that you should start simple with a focus on one or two sounds at first. Children should begin by practicing isolating the initial sound of words with the eventual goal of producing these sounds as well. It is crucial to make sure that you don't confuse the sounds in words with the letters that represent them. Many letters can make more than one sound (e.g., the letter *c* can make a hard /c/ as in camel, but can also make a soft sound as in ceiling). Finally, keep it fun and interactive. There are many engaging books and activities that can emphasize alliteration!

ALLITERATION ACTIVITY IDEAS: SUMMARY

(activities appropriate for younger children are listed first)

Use pictures, objects, and writing materials
Sort objects and pictures into labeled "mailbags"
Match picture cards depicting same initial sound ("Sound-tration")
Adapt rhyming activities (e.g., cube) to focus on initial sound
Connect target phoneme(s) with letter(s) using plastic letters, air or carpet writing, or writing on paper

Phonological awareness as a whole focuses on the sounds of our language. Below we present a set of general phonologic goals for emergent readers. The objective (beyond preschool and into kindergarten and beyond) is to connect phonological awareness with letter recognition and writing to reinforce the correspondence between sounds and the letters that represent them. Understanding this correspondence provides children with the key to "unlock" the door to literacy—to prepare children to successfully read and write.

PHONOLOGICAL AWARENESS GOALS

Segment (e.g., clap) sentences into words, words into syllables
Recognize and produce rhymes
Match words on basis of same initial sound (alliteration)
Match on basis of a few (four to twelve) initial sounds, writing down letter for some of the sounds

PHONOLOGICAL AWARENESS RISK

Phonological awareness refers to the ability to attend to how spoken words sound and includes a variety of different skills. Difficulty in some of these areas may indicate that a child is at risk for reading difficulties. However, many of these skills do require some instruction, so you cannot assume that a child is having difficulty if the child simply has not been exposed to the skill in question. For example, children who have problems recognizing and producing rhyme even after it has been introduced (via books, songs, and activities) may be at particular risk. These children may need more explicit instruction than others in phoneme awareness. With explicit instruction, these children can usually learn how to read. The development of alliteration (the ability to attend to the beginning sound of a word) does benefit from the knowledge of letters and words. In preschool and kindergarten, the ability to match on the basis of initial sounds predicts later reading success. However, failure to do this means very little. Children need guidance in attending to initial phonemes and failure may simply indicate a lack of guidance.

RECOMMENDED BOOKS FOR PHONOLOGICAL AWARENESS

I Like Myself	Karen Beaumont
"Slowly, Slowly, Slowly," Said the Sloth	Eric Carle
Jamberry	Bruce Degen
Slop Goes the Soup	Pamela Duncan Edwards
Some Smug Slug	Pamela Duncan Edwards
This Jazz Man	Karen Ehrhardt
Bebe Goes Shopping	Susan Middleton Elya
Say Hola to Spanish	Susan Middleton Elya
Say Hola to Spanish at the Circus	Susan Middleton Elya
Is Your Mama a Llama?	Deborah Guarino
Many Marvelous Monsters	Ed Heck
Wemberly Worried	Kevin Henkes
Hush! A Thai Lullaby	Minfong Ho
Violet's Music	Angela Johnson
Roar and More	Karla Kuskin
Squeak, Rumble, Whomp! Whomp! *Whomp!*	Wynton Marsalis
Dinosaur A–Z	Roger Priddy
Charlie Parker Played Be Bop	Chris Raschka
Rattletrap Car	Phyllis Root
Sing a Song of Popcorn	Beatrice Schenk de Regniers et al., eds.
Dr. Seuss's ABC	Dr. Seuss (Theodor Geisel)
Fox in Socks	Dr. Seuss
One Fish, Two Fish, Red Fish, Blue Fish	Dr. Seuss
There's a Wocket in My Pocket	Dr. Seuss
Sheep in a Jeep	Nancy Shaw
Falling Up	Shel Silverstein
Pigs in Pajamas	Maggie Smith
Tops & Bottoms	Janet Stevens
Bear Snores On	Karma Wilson
Chinese Mother Goose Rhymes	Robert Wyndham

HOW-TO ACTIVITY: Syllable Sort

For the syllable sort, first create picture cards with words that are of one, two, or three syllables. The cards could be simple line drawings or photos cut from magazines glued to cardboard. The pictures could come from any domain you and your child are interested in as long as they vary in the number of syllables. You could even incorporate a theme if you are working on one in a classroom. For example, a spring theme could include words like *frog, egg, flower, rabbit,* or *butterfly.* Finally, you will need to create category cards labeled with the numbers 1, 2, and 3.

Start by identifying and naming each of the pictures (this could be done with the children producing the words). Then have the child(ren) clap the number of syllables for each word and place it into the proper category.

HOW-TO ACTIVITY: Odd Sound Out

For the odd sound out activity you will be focusing on the initial sound in words. First, create a set of picture cards that have some words that share an initial sound, with one word that is the odd one out. For example, you could have a picture of a snake, a star, and a spoon, and then the odd one out could be a nest. You should have several sets of cards with a different initial sound for each. Present the set of cards to each child (if working in a group). First, have the children name each picture and then have them choose the one that is the odd sound out.

HOW-TO ACTIVITY: Sound Search

This activity could be done anywhere the child is surrounded by lots of different objects, peoples, or animals (at the grocery store, at preschool, at the zoo, etc.). Choose a sound to search for in your environment and have the child identify all the things that he or she can find that begin with that sound (if working with multiple children have them take turns seeing if they can find objects that start with the sound). Make sure to repeat the sound several times, and have the child slowly say the name for the item that he or she has identified, isolating that initial sound. This can be repeated multiple times with various initial sounds.

HOW-TO ACTIVITY: Rhyming Hot Potato or Rhyming Lineup

Use Rhyming Words from Books or Make Up Your Own

This activity can be done inside or outside with a group of children. You would first create a set of pictures of words that are easy for children to match with a rhyme (these could be pictures from some of the books with rhyming words that you have already read). Have the children sit in a circle and play music (that you can easily start and stop) as they pass a ball around the circle. When the music stops the child who has the ball names the picture that you show her and then comes up with a word that rhymes with it. Then you can start the music again and continue to pass the ball.

You could also use the same set of pictures and have the children take turns naming a rhyming word. One way is to have the children line up single file. The child at the front of the line picks one of the pictures and has to name a rhyming word. Once that child's turn is over have her quickly go to the end of the line, and let the next child take a turn. When a picture is matched correctly with a rhyme, put it in a discard pile. If the rhyme is incorrect, put it back in the pile and let the child select another picture. To make it more fun, time the children to see how quickly they can get all the pictures in the discard pile.

REFERENCES

Bradley, Lynette, and Peter Bryant. "Categorizing Sounds and Learning to Read: A Causal Connection." *Nature* 301 (1983): 419–21.

———. *Rhyme and Reason in Reading and Spelling.* Ann Arbor: University of Michigan Press, 1985.

Bryant, Peter, M. MacLean, Lynette Bradley, and J. Crossland. "Rhyme and Alliteration, Phoneme Detection and Learning to Read." *Developmental Psychology* 26, no. 3 (1990): 429–38.

Liberman, Isabelle Y., Donald Shankweiler, Linda Camp, Benita Blachman, and Michele Werfelman. "Steps toward Literacy." In *Auditory Processing and Lan-*

guage: Clinical and Research Perspectives, edited by Philip Levinson and Christine Sloan. New York: Grune & Stratton, 1980.

Lonigan, Christopher, Stephen Burgess, Jason Anthony, and Theodore Barker. "Development of Phonological Sensitivity in 2- to 5-Year-Old Children." *Journal of Educational Psychology* 90, no. 2 (1998): 294–311.

Shankweiler, Donald, and Anne E. Fowler. "Questions People Ask about the Role of Phonological Processes in Learning to Read." *Reading and Writing: An Interdisciplinary Journal* 17, no. 5 (2004): 483–515.

Whitehurst, Grover, and Christopher Lonigan. "Child Development and Emergent Literacy." *Child Development* 69, no. 3 (1998): 848–72.

BIBLIOGRAPHY

Beaumont, Karen. *I Like Myself.* Illus. by David Catrow. New York: Harcourt, 2004. 32 p.

Carle, Eric. *"Slowly, Slowly, Slowly," Said the Sloth.* Illus. by the author. New York: Puffin, 2002. 32 p.

Degen, Bruce. *Jamberry.* Illus. by the author. New York: Harper & Row, 1983. 32 p.

Edwards, Pamela Duncan. *Slop Goes the Soup.* Illus. by Henry Cole. New York: Hyperion, 2001. 32 p.

——. *Some Smug Slug.* Illus. by Henry Cole. New York: HarperCollins, 1996. 32 p.

Ehrhardt, Karen. *This Jazz Man.* Illus. by R. G. Roth. New York: Harcourt, 2006. 32 p.

Elya, Susan Middleton. *Bebe Goes Shopping.* Illus. by Steven Salerno. New York: Harcourt, 2006. 40 p.

——. *Say Hola to Spanish.* Illus. by Loretta Lopez. New York: Lee & Low, 1996. 32 p.

——. *Say Hola to Spanish at the Circus.* Illus. by Loretta Lopez. New York: Lee & Low, 2000. 32 p.

Guarino, Deborah. *Is Your Mama a Llama?* Illus. by Steven Kellogg. New York: Scholastic, 1989. 32 p.

Heck, Ed. *Many Marvelous Monsters.* Illus. by the author. New York: Penguin, 2010. 16 p.

Henkes, *Wemberly Worried.* Illus. by the author. New York: Greenwillow, 2000. 32 p.

Ho, Minfong. *Hush! A Thai Lullaby.* Illus. by Holly Meade. New York: Scholastic, 1996. 32 p.

Johnson, Angela. *Violet's Music*. Illus. by Laura Huliska-Beith. New York: Penguin, 2004. 32 p.

Kuskin, Karla. *Roar and More*. Illus. by the author. New York: Harper, 1956. 48 p.

Marsalis, Wynton. *Squeak, Rumble, Whomp! Whomp! Whomp!* Illus. by Paul Rogers. Cambridge, Mass.: Candlewick, 2012. 40 p.

Priddy, Roger. *Dinosaur A–Z*. Illus. by the author. New York: St. Martin's, 2004. 32 p.

Raschka, Chris. *Charlie Parker Played Be Bop*. Illus. by the author. New York: Orchard, 1992. 32 p.

Root, Phyllis. *Rattletrap Car*. Illus. by Jill Barton. Cambridge, Mass.: Candlewick, 2001. 40 p.

Schenk de Regniers, Beatrice, Eva Moore, Mary Michaels White, and Jan Carr, eds. *Sing a Song of Popcorn*. Illus. by Maurice Sendak, Leo and Diane Dillon, Richard Egielski, Arnold Lobel, Marcia Brown, and Margot Zemach. New York: Scholastic, 1988. 160 p.

Seuss, Dr. *Dr. Seuss's ABC*. Illus. by the author. New York: Random House, 1963. 32 p.

——. *Fox in Socks*. Illus. by the author. New York: Random House, 1965. 62 p.

——. *One Fish, Two Fish, Red Fish, Blue Fish*. Illus. by the author. New York: Random House, 1960. 63 p.

——. *There's a Wocket in My Pocket*. Illus. by the author. New York: Houghton Mifflin, 1974. 36 p.

Shaw, Nancy. *Sheep in a Jeep*. Illus. by Margot Apple. New York: Houghton Mifflin Harcourt, 1997. 26 p.

Silverstein, Shel. *Falling Up*. Illus. by the author. New York: HarperCollins, 1996. 184 p.

Smith, Maggie. *Pigs in Pajamas*. Illus. by the author. New York: Knopf, 2012. 32 p.

Stevens, Janet. *Tops & Bottoms*. Illus. by the author. San Diego, Calif.: Harcourt, 1995. 40 p.

Wilson, Karma. *Bear Snores On*. Illus. by Jane Chapman. New York: Simon & Schuster, 2001. 34 p.

Wyndham, Robert. *Chinese Mother Goose Rhymes*. Illus. by Ed Young. New York: Putnam & Grosset, 1968. 48 p.

6

VOCABULARY

The limits of my language are the limits of my mind. All I know is what I have words for.

—Ludwig Wittgenstein

A s has been noted in several sections of this book, including the previous chapter, an emphasis on spoken language is crucial for early literacy development. In chapter 5 we highlighted the role of phonological awareness (knowledge of the sounds of spoken language) in reading success. In this chapter, the emphasis will be on knowledge of the *meaning* of spoken words as a critical foundation for reading. As in previous chapters, we will suggest some books and activities that can help to foster vocabulary learning in the young children in your life.

WHAT IS VOCABULARY?

In general, vocabulary refers to knowledge of word meanings. However, this term can be further broken down into two components: *receptive* and *expressive* vocabulary. A child's receptive vocabulary refers to all the words that the child recognizes or understands when heard. For example, we might test receptive vocabulary by saying a word and asking a child to point to a picture of that word. Expressive vocabulary, on the other hand, refers to the words that a child can produce to label the objects around him or her. Expressive vocabulary is typically measured by showing a child a picture and asking the child to name the object or action presented. While both of these components of vocabulary contribute to reading development, it is a child's ability to *produce* the correct labels for the world around him or her (or the child's expressive vocabulary) that is the strongest predictor of reading success (Scarborough, 1998). Given the crucial role of expressive vocabulary, this skill will be the emphasis of this chapter.

WHY IS EXPRESSIVE VOCABULARY
IMPORTANT FOR READING?

There are many reasons why vocabulary is important for reading success. In general, vocabulary, whether it is receptive or expressive, provides a window into a child's access to different types of experiences. A child who has gone to the zoo might learn the word *tortoise*, for example. Knowing the word, and perhaps having some background knowledge about tortoises will aid a child's comprehension, or understanding, when reading or being read to. It is also much easier to recognize a word or sound it out when reading if you have the word in your own spoken vocabulary. Phonological awareness depends on accurate pronunciation of words, and it is much harder to accurately pronounce a word if you have never heard it before!

WHAT IS IMPORTANT WHEN FOCUSING ON EXPRESSIVE VOCABULARY?

Three facets of expressive vocabulary are important to emphasize. The first is that we want the words that children know to be well defined conceptually. This is crucial to both written and spoken language comprehension. For example, a child who uses the word *chair* for *couch* might be missing a critical piece of information in understanding that a chair is generally for one person whereas a couch can seat more. The second is that accurate and precise pronunciation of words is important for mapping written (alphabetic) representation onto spoken representation. A child needs to be able to clearly say a word out loud in order to then be able to transfer that phonological knowledge when reading. For example, a child who mispronounces the word *giraffe* as "traf" does not have a precise sound-based representation of that word. It would be hard to read or spell giraffe (that is, find it among other words) with this imprecise phonological representation.

The final important factor to emphasize in vocabulary knowledge is accessibility of the words. Children must be able to access the meaning of a word across a range of contexts. For example, a child who reads about a runner taking a lap around a track may complain that we sit in a lap. The more connections a child has for a given word, the faster he or she will be able to access the meaning. The ultimate goal of reading is comprehension, or understanding, of what is read. When children know words, both in terms of their pronunciations and their multiple meanings, this will only serve to enhance their understanding of what they are reading.

HOW DO CHILDREN ACQUIRE EXPRESSIVE VOCABULARY?

The short answer to the question above is that children acquire vocabulary by being spoken to. Hearing and engaging in oral language is the base from which literacy is built. From as early in development as toddlerhood, children have been shown to learn new vocabulary from their surrounding environment (the words being spoken by their parents and caregivers). Additionally, the faster a child can identify the words that she knows when they are spoken to her, the more attention she can pay to learning *new* words. This means that the more different words children hear and know, then the more likely they are to learn new words when they hear them. Research has shown that both English- and Spanish-learning toddlers who were faster at recognizing familiar words in toddlerhood (at eighteen months) had larger vocabularies at age two and scored higher on standardized tests of language and cognition in kindergarten and elementary school (Weisleder and Fernald, 2013). This finding underscores the key importance of oral language in vocabulary and literacy development. One of the easiest things that you can do to foster expressive vocabulary is to talk with your children. This does not need to be complicated. You can label the everyday objects in their environment, such as naming the fruits and vegetables you find at the grocery store, telling them about your day, explaining what you are doing as you help them put on their shoes. All of these small steps will serve to further introduce them to the sounds and meanings of the words in their language.

INTRODUCING VOCABULARY USING BOOKS

While talking with children is very important, books are also one of the richest sources of diverse vocabulary (Biemiller, 2001; Chall, Jacobs, and Baldwin, 1990). Reading to children is a wonderful way to build a child's expressive vocabulary. However, like the other skills introduced in this book, we cannot leave vocabulary learning to chance. We must make a conscious and intentional effort to choose the right books and the right type of words to introduce. Additionally, to have an impact on understanding the text in books, vocabulary instruction itself must be rich and detailed, which means many encounters with new words (four or five times minimum) (Beck, McKeown, and Omanson, 1987). Children should be encouraged to produce the new words that they learn, as the best way to learn is through active engagement. Exposing children to new words in multiple ways will also help to ensure that they are really learning the words in a deep and meaningful way. You can ask children to relate new words to words that they already know or to experiences that they have had. Continuing to use these new words outside of a single vocabulary "lesson" will also help to reinforce their meaning.

One of the more challenging aspects of fostering vocabulary learning is deciding which words to focus on. Because there are many words that children may not know, how do you decide where to begin? To help you choose the right vocabulary words to introduce to children, researcher Isabel Beck identifies three kinds of words that children will encounter in books (Beck, McKeown, and Kucan, 2002). Beck says that you should be like Goldilocks, selecting to focus on words that are "not too easy, not too hard, but just right." Beck refers to these words as falling with three different tiers. Easy words (often referred to as Tier 1) are ones that most children already know or that can easily be taught with a picture (such as *flower*) or a synonym (such as *hare* for *rabbit*). Tier 1 words are typically common, frequently used words, such as *baby*, *run*, or *happy*. Preschoolers are already acquiring these words and are doing so at a rapid pace. Thus, for most children Tier 1 words are "too easy." On the other end are Tier 3 words, which are potentially "too hard." These are words that indicate a specialized knowledge, words like *wallow*, *paddock*, and *rafters* (all of which appear in *Barnyard Banter* by Denise Fleming). These words are less common, limited to specific domains or areas (such as farming or astronomy) and are best learned within that content domain. For most children we want to focus on Tier 2 words, those that are "just right." These are words that are useful and "higher level," such as words like *emergency*, *demand*, or *impatient* (all appear in the book *Click, Clack, Moo: Cows That Type* by Doreen Cronin). These Tier 2 words are ordinary words for mature language users, but sophisticated for younger children (e.g., as adults the word *generous* might be used instead of *nice*; however, *generous* would be a sophisticated word for a young child). Tier 2 words are also high utility—meaning that they are useful across many different contexts. For example, the word *ingest* is a higher-level word that a young child may not know; however, it means little more than to eat. However, *devour* (meaning to "take something in with enthusiasm") can be used in many different situations such as devouring a book or a meal. Finally, Tier 2 words are conceptually appropriate—meaning that children may understand the general concept (e.g., *devour* for eating), but may lack precision and specificity. Introduction and familiarity of these Tier 2 words provides more sophisticated vocabulary for most children.

GENERAL PRACTICES TO ENHANCE VOCABULARY VIA BOOK READING

Many early books provide very little in the way of vocabulary enrichment (using mostly those Tier 1 words). However, you also do not want to choose books where many of the words are unfamiliar. Instead, in order to enrich vocabulary, select volumes where children recognize *most* of the words. Books with an engaging yet straightforward story line will provide a solid context for target vocabulary words. In general, you should attempt to focus on three high-utility, Tier 2 words per reading. Read the book multiple times, as this will allow you to introduce a few new words with each reading. You can also do this with different versions of same story, like *Henny Penny*. You can introduce the older, more simple and familiar story first (about a chicken who warns that the sky is falling) and then use more modern versions that incorporate expanded vocabulary (such as the version by Jane Wattenberg).

ACTIVITIES TO SUPPORT EXPRESSIVE VOCABULARY

Books combined with some creative activities can be utilized to help develop a rich expressive vocabulary. One activity is to act out verbs worth learning, which actively engages children with the stories found in books and in learning new words. For example, *Mr. Gumpy's Outing* by John Burningham contains many descriptive active words that children might not know. In this story Mr. Gumpy takes a ride in his small boat and is joined by various troublemaking animals and children. The book could be read a few times, and by the second or third reading children could participate by repeating the phrase "Yes, but don't bleat, trample or squabble." This will help both with understanding the meaning of the words and gives the children a chance to produce the words. You can also have children act out verbs such as "squabble" introduced in *Mr. Gumpy's Outing*; "stared" and "roared" could be acted out from *Officer Buckle and Gloria* by Peggy Rathmann.

Furthermore, you can ask children to relate a new word to their own life. For example, in the story *Click, Clack, Moo: Cows That Type* by Doreen Cronin, the word *furious* is introduced. At the end of the story, you can define the word for the children by saying, "Furious means very, very mad" then, expand by asking children if they or anyone they know has ever been furious. The children can explain and act out their answers. (Other words from this story that would work well are *emergency, demand,* and *impatient.*) Make sure that you provide feedback so that the child is using the word accurately.

Another activity to foster expressive vocabulary is to take advantage of a new word that is repeated several times in one book. Evidence shows the best way to teach a word is to use it multiple times in different contexts (Biemiller, 2001; Chall, Jacobs, and Baldwin, 1990). For example, *Tops & Bottoms* by Janet Stevens uses the word *harvest* five times. Although this is not a critical word for four-year-olds, it is central to this story. The reader could explain what harvest means in the first or second mention ("when you pick the vegetables") and from then ask the child to produce it ("When it was time for the . . . harvest"). This book would also lend itself to a flannel board retelling acting out the words *plant, water, weed, grow,* and *harvest.* Each time you use the words you could incorporate a different vegetable and have the children produce as well as listen to the vocabulary words. A few other books that use word repetition that could enhance a child's vocabulary are *Delicious!* by Helen Cooper (using the words *delicious, scrumptious,* and *nutritious*), *The Growing Story* by Ruth Krauss (using the word *grow* in several different contexts), and *Hurty Feelings* by Helen Lester (using the words *fragile, sturdy,* and *solid*).

The concept sort is another activity that supports expressive vocabulary. In the case of *Tops & Bottoms*, you could make picture cards for foods to sort. First, you would model the sorting of foods according to certain criteria such as whether we harvest the tops or the bottoms. Children could either participate as a group or independently name the pictures and justify their sorts orally. You could then expand using the same pictures from the book and include other foods so that children can sort them into other categories (e.g., fruits/vegetables or colors). Again, the goal is to increase familiarity with a vocabulary word, expanding the child's conceptual knowledge while also promoting development of the phonological representations of the words by having them say the word out loud.

Whether it is nature, animals, dinosaurs, or trains, choosing books about a topic of particular interest to a child will engage the child and provide opportunities for exposure to new vocabulary. One example of books that support vocabulary development are those that have nonfiction information, such as *The Water Hole* by Graeme Base, which uses words like *lapping* or *squawking*, and *Commotion in the Ocean* by Giles Andreae, which introduces scientific vocabulary to children. These books would work well to introduce vocabulary while at the same time adding to the child's background knowledge about the world. For example, a book such as *Bird, Butterfly, Eel* by James Prosek introduces several rich vocabulary words (e.g., *journey* and *cycle*) in a story about animals that migrate from north to south and back again. The vocabulary words could be introduced in the context of a simple explanation about why animals migrate.

EXPRESSIVE VOCABULARY ACTIVITY IDEAS: SUMMARY

Act out verbs from book
Relate words to child's own life
Make use of repetition of vocabulary words
Use nonfiction or informational books to introduce vocabulary
Concept sort

EXPRESSIVE VOCABULARY GOALS

By kindergarten entry, children should be able to:

- Learn and use new words daily
- Sort relationships among words in knowledge domains

- Recognize that some words go by more than one name: "Fluffy," cat, pet, animal
- Use diverse word choices—*happy, surprised, thrilled*, etc.
- Work toward interest in and enthusiasm for words

VOCABULARY RISK

Typically achieving children learn approximately three thousand new words per year (Nagy, 1988) although estimates can range from one thousand to five thousand (White, Graves, and Slater, 1990). Working with all children to build vocabulary knowledge will be crucial to their reading and academic success. However, it is especially important to help those children who are on the lower end of the scale. As we have mentioned before, initially children are learning to read, but as they develop they will be *reading to learn*. Vocabulary deficits will certainly impact a child's ability to comprehend more complex reading material. For example, children with low vocabulary need to solidly establish two or three words a day to be ready for fourth-grade material by the fourth grade (Adams, 1990). Even though this is the case, research indicates there is currently minimal instruction in vocabulary in the early elementary grades; teachers typically do not focus on explicit vocabulary instruction until third or fourth grade, when it is already too late for children to catch up (Biemiller, 2001). Books, not surprisingly, are the richest source of diverse vocabulary. As we have outlined above there are some easy ways to enrich vocabulary development (Biemiller and Boote, 2006; Chall, Jacobs, and Baldwin, 1990). Some children, especially those who have very limited basic vocabulary skills, may need extra support and would benefit by working with some easier books that are filled with simple vocabulary connecting to various themes such as those by Richard Scarry. Some good examples are *Richard Scarry's Best Word Book Ever* or *Cars, Trucks, and Things That Go*. For younger children a good picture dictionary could also be helpful. There are many good examples available, such as *Scholastic First Picture Dictionary* by Scholastic or *My First 1000 Words* by Publications International.

RECOMMENDED BOOKS FOR EXPRESSIVE VOCABULARY

Commotion in the Ocean	Giles Andreae
Giraffes Can't Dance	Giles Andreae
Max's Words	Kate Banks
Animalia	Graeme Base
The Water Hole	Graeme Base
Mr. Gumpy's Outing	John Burningham
Big, Bigger, Biggest	Nancy Coffelt
Delicious!	Helen Cooper
Click, Clack, Moo: Cows That Type	Doreen Cronin
The Big Book of Dinosaurs: A First Book for Young Children	DK
Barnyard Banter	Denise Fleming
Henny Penny	Paul Galdone
The Growing Story	Ruth Krauss
Hurty Feelings	Helen Lester
I'm Fast!	Kate and Jim McMullan
I Stink	Kate and Jim McMullan
Bird, Butterfly, Eel	James Prosek
My First 1000 Words	Publications International
Officer Buckle and Gloria	Peggy Rathmann
Cars, Trucks, and Things That Go	Richard Scarry
Richard Scarry's Best Word Book Ever	Richard Scarry
Scholastic First Picture Dictionary	Scholastic
Tops & Bottoms	Janet Stevens
How Do Dinosaurs Clean Their Rooms?	Jane Yolen and Mark Teague
How Do Dinosaurs Say Good Night?	Jane Yolen and Mark Teague

HOW-TO ACTIVITY: Using Children's Special Interests to Develop Vocabulary

Activities to Pair with Special Interest Books: Take a Trip!
If the child in your life is interested in animals, books like *The Water Hole* or *Animalia*, both by Graeme Base, include words like *devouring*, *lapping*, or *babbling*. These books show many different types of animals that may be found in a nearby zoo, such as an armadillo, a tiger, a toucan.

- After reading animal books with your child, take a trip to the zoo and find some of the animals in her or his favorite book.
- Read from the signs at the zoo and point out the names of animals and words that describe their habits and habitats.
- Recall some of the language from the books when you visit. For example, in *The Water Hole,* the toucans "squawk." Do they make that sound when you see them in the zoo? The tigers lap water in *The Water Hole.* Do you see them lapping in their habitat on your visit?
- Model use of the vocabulary words you have chosen, and encourage your child to use the words as you talk about your trip, while planning the trip, during the visit, and after the visit.

This approach could also work well with children who have an interest in the ocean or in sea animals. Reading a book like *Commotion in the Ocean* by Giles Andreae could then be followed up with a visit to an aquarium, or if your child's interest is in dinosaurs, a book like *The Big Book of Dinosaurs: A First Book for Young Children* by DK, *How Do Dinosaurs Say Good Night?* or *How Do Dinosaurs Clean Their Rooms?*, both by Jane Yolen and Mark Teague, would be great to read before a visit to a natural history museum to see the dinosaur fossils. Similarly, if your child has an interest in trains, you could read *I'm Fast* by Kate and Jim McMullan and then venture to a train station and watch the trains arrive and depart, notice the words on the schedules, and read the signs in the station.

However, using a child's interests to build vocabulary via books need not require a trip. If your child is particularly interested in trucks, for example, then you could read *I Stink!* by Kate and Jim McMullan. This book includes lots of great words, such as *appetite*, *stinky*, and *squeals*. Rather than leaving your home, you could read *I Stink!* and then watch your local garbage truck as it collects your trash. When the truck comes, you can discuss what you see and hear based on the language you have learned in the book.

HOW-TO ACTIVITY: Vocabulary Concept Sort

Using the Book Tops & Bottoms *by Janet Stevens*

- Create picture cards of foods that appear in the book to sort
- Place the pictures into sorts, in piles, or in paper bags or mailboxes
- Model sorting of foods according to different criteria, for example:

  Aboveground (e.g., lettuce, celery)
  Belowground (e.g., beets, carrots)
  By color (green/not green)
  Fruits vs. vegetables

- Children say the word out loud and sort into the proper container

An optional additional activity is to paste pictures of fruits and/or vegetables on a board and have children provide the label, supporting their knowledge of vocabulary.

HOW-TO ACTIVITY: Word Collection

Using the Book Max's Words *by Kate Banks*

The title character in the book has two older brothers who have collections (stamps and coins). Max wants a collection, so he decides to collect words. He cuts them out of newspapers and magazines and writes them down on pieces of paper. Soon his collection is big enough that he can write a whole story.

In this activity, first read the book together with the children. Then you can encourage them to start collecting words. If you are working with a group of children, the collection could be displayed on a word wall (a big sheet of paper prominently placed where you can add new vocabulary words that have been introduced). With a single child you could keep a small notebook to record your collection.

In keeping with some of the principles discussed above, you can refer to these words often and point them out at times when they are relevant. Or, when you add a new word you could take the time to go back and review some of the old ones. Encourage the children, like Max, to use the words in a story that they write together or alone.

HOW-TO ACTIVITY: Synonyms and Comparisons

Using the Book Big, Bigger, Biggest *by Nancy Coffelt*
In this book, different animals are used to illustrate that different words can have the same meaning (known as synonyms). Additionally, it illustrates word comparisons (big, bigger, biggest). For example, a hippopotamus says, "I'm big. I'm large. I'm huge. I'm jumbo." On the next page a whale says, "I'm bigger. I'm gigantic. I'm immense. I'm enormous." Finally, a very large dinosaur says, "I'm biggest. I'm mammoth. I'm humongous. I'm colossal."

While this book contains too many vocabulary words for one lesson, it is an excellent introduction to the idea that many words share similar meanings.

One way to use this would be to pick one of the words and start out by having children list as many words that they can think of that share a meaning. Make a list of the words they come up with. You could then read that section together with the children to see if they came up with some of the words that are in the book.

To work with comparisons you could have them generate things that fit in each category. For example, if you used the word *small*, have them name things that are small. Then have them name things that are smaller than the examples they just came up with. Finally, have them come up with items that fit in the smallest category.

HOW-TO ACTIVITY: Acting Out Verbs

Using the Book Giraffes Can't Dance *by Giles Andreae*
This is a story about a giraffe that gets made fun of by the other animals because he can't dance. It turns out that he can, but he just needs to find the right music. This book is rich in vocabulary words, many of which are action verbs such as *sway, swish, shuffle, skip,* and *prance.*

In this activity you could first introduce the words and their meaning to the children as you read the story together. After reading, have the children get up and see if they can demonstrate the words' meaning by acting out the movements. Put on some music and see if the children can sway, skip, and prance to the sounds. You could also have the children watch the Scholastic Interactive animated video of the story being read, which also includes some music matched to the timing of the action (http://vimeo.com/33829782). This activity engages multiple modes through the storybook reading and watching and through the children's movement.

REFERENCES

Adams, Marilyn Jager. *Beginning to Read: Thinking and Learning about Print.* Cambridge, Mass.: MIT Press, 1990.

Beck, Isabel, Margaret McKeown, and Linda Kucan. *Bringing Words to Life: Robust Vocabulary Instruction.* New York: Guilford, 2002.

Beck, Isabel, Margaret McKeown, and Richard Omanson. "The Effects and Uses of Diverse Vocabulary Instructional Techniques." In *The Nature of Vocabulary Acquisition*, edited by Margaret McKeown and Mary E. Curtis. Hillsdale, N.J.: Erlbaum, 1987.

Biemiller, Andrew. "Teaching Vocabulary: Early, Direct, and Sequential." *American Educator* 25, no. 1 (2001): 24–28.

Biemiller, Andrew, and Catherine Boote. "An Effective Method for Building Meaning Vocabulary in Primary Grades." *Journal of Educational Psychology* 98, no. 1 (2006): 44–62.

Chall, Jeanne, Vicki Jacobs, and Luke Baldwin. *The Reading Crisis: Why Poor Children Fall Behind.* Cambridge, Mass.: Harvard University Press, 1990.

Nagy, William E. *Teaching Vocabulary to Improve Reading Comprehension.* Urbana, Ill.: National Council of Teachers of English, 1988.

Scarborough, Hollis. "Early Identification of Children at Risk for Reading Disabilities: Phonological Awareness and Some Other Promising Predictors." In *Specific Reading Disability: A View of the Spectrum*, edited by Bruce K. Shapiro, Pasquale J. Accardo, and Arnold J. Capute, 75–119. Timonium, Md.: York, 1998.

Weisleder, Adriana, and Anne Fernald. "Talking to Children Matters: Early Language Experience Strengthens Processing and Builds Vocabulary." *Psychological Science* 24, no. 11 (2013): 2143–52.

White, Thomas G., Michael F. Graves, and Wayne H. Slater. "Growth of Reading Vocabulary in Diverse Elementary Schools: Decoding and Word Meaning." *Journal of Educational Psychology* 82, no. 2 (1990): 281–90.

BIBLIOGRAPHY

Andreae, Giles. *Commotion in the Ocean.* Illus. by David Wojtowycz. Wilton, Conn.: Tiger Tales, 2002. 32 p.

——. *Giraffes Can't Dance.* Illus. by Guy Parker-Rees. London: Orchard, 1999. 32 p.

Banks, Kate. *Max's Words.* Illus. by Boris Kulikov. New York: Farrar, Straus and Giroux, 2006. 32 p.

Base, Graeme. *Animalia.* Illus. by the author. New York: Abrams, 1993. 32 p.

——. *The Water Hole.* Illus. by the author. New York: Abrams, 2001. 32 p.

Burningham, John. *Mr. Gumpy's Outing.* Illus. by the author. New York: Holt, Rinehart, and Winston, 1970. 32 p.

Coffelt, Nancy. *Big, Bigger, Biggest.* Illus. by the author. New York: Holt, 2009. 32 p.

Cooper, Helen. *Delicious!* Illus. by the author. New York: Doubleday, 2006. 32 p.

Cronin, Doreen. *Click, Clack, Moo: Cows That Type.* Illus. by Betsy Lewin. New York: Simon & Schuster, 2000. 42 p.

DK Publishing. *The Big Book of Dinosaurs: A First Book for Young Children.* New York: DK, 1993. 32 p.

Fleming, Denise. *Barnyard Banter.* Illus. by the author. New York: Holt, 1994. 32 p.

Galdone, Paul. *Henny Penny.* Illus. by the author. New York: Seabury, 1968. 32 p.

Krauss, Ruth. *The Growing Story.* Illus. by Helen Oxenbury. New York: Harper-Collins, 1947. 40 p.

Lester, Helen. *Hurty Feelings.* Illus. by Lynn Munsinger. Boston: Houghton Mifflin, 2007. 32 p.

McMullan, Kate, and Jim McMullan. *I'm Fast!* Illus. by Jim McMullan. New York: HarperCollins, 2012. 40 p.

——. *I Stink!* Illus. by Jim McMullan. New York: HarperCollins, 2002. 40 p.

Prosek, James. *Bird, Butterfly, Eel.* Illus. by the author. New York: Simon & Schuster, 2009. 32 p.

Publications International, eds. *My First 1000 Words.* Lincolnwood, Ill.: Publications International, 2005. 96 p.

Rathmann, Peggy. *Officer Buckle and Gloria.* Illus. by the author. New York: Putnam, 1995. 40 p.

Scarry, Richard. *Cars, Trucks, and Things That Go.* Illus. by the author. New York: Random House, 1998. 72 p.

———. *Richard Scarry's Best Word Book Ever.* Illus. by the author. New York: Random House, 1963. 70 p.

Scholastic. *Scholastic First Picture Dictionary.* New York: Scholastic, 2009. 96 p.

Stevens, Janet. *Tops & Bottoms.* Illus. by the author. San Diego, Calif.: Harcourt, 1995. 40 p.

Yolen, Jane, and Mark Teague. *How Do Dinosaurs Clean Their Rooms?* Illus. by Mark Teague. New York: Blue Sky, 2004. 12 p.

———. *How Do Dinosaurs Say Good Night?* Illus. by Mark Teague. New York: Blue Sky, 2000. 40 p.

7

DECONTEXTUALIZED LANGUAGE

Reading is important because, if you can read, you can learn any-thing about everything and everything about anything.

—Tomie dePaola

In the previous chapter we discussed the importance of vocabulary, especially expressive vocabulary, in emerging literacy. Often, however, the vocabulary found in books is language without a context. In spoken language, if a child hears a word that he doesn't know he may be able to figure it out by referring to the surrounding physical or social environment. However, the language used in books doesn't always provide enough information to determine the meaning of a word or sentence. Because of this, readers must become skilled at gaining meaning from language without other supports (such as pictures) and in using language to express ideas and situations that go beyond the "here and now." We now turn to the progression of language development from basic speaking and listening skills for communication established in the home environment through the more complex and precise language needed in the classroom and the world outside of the home and finally, to the complex, decontextualized language found in books.

DECONTEXTUALIZED LANGUAGE

Children begin learning language at home. While the home language environment can be rich and meaningful to the child, language used in the home usually differs greatly from language used in classrooms and books. Generally, language used in the home is very context dependent. This means that the children are talking about topics that are meaningful to them and that are grounded in their immediate environment. For example, a child can easily discuss her new shoes by saying, "Look what I got" (pointing to new shoes). Additionally, while a parent may have little problem understanding a child who says /okopus/ for octopus when an octopus toy or image is present, once the child moves out of the familiar environment he may have difficulty being understood. While the language used at home serves an essential function in that children can easily communicate their wants and needs, very often this language is simpler than either classroom or book language. Thus, one of the first challenges a young child faces at kindergarten and later is to transition from home language to the more decontextualized language used at school and in books.

When children move from the home environment to the classroom, language becomes more precise and complex and children must be able to understand and use concepts and language forms that are not well grounded in their everyday life. For example, even in a basic science unit where children are learning about the seasons, the vocabulary being used (e.g., seasons and cycles) and the topics that are discussed (e.g., changes in the weather and animals migrating to warmer climates) require an increasing level of sophistication. The language that is used in books often adds still another layer to the levels of language that children must understand. While many children's books support language learning pictorially (e.g., using illustrations to support new vocabulary), children must work toward understanding text without pictures. Thus, decontextualized language refers to the exclusive use of symbol systems to represent the world. In this way, words alone must "paint the picture" sufficiently to enable older children to understand what they hear and read. Books are a natural way to convey the concept of decontextualized language.

FOSTERING DECONTEXTUALIZED LANGUAGE VIA OPEN-ENDED QUESTIONS

Language, like many skills, can't be learned just by watching others. In order to learn language, children have to actively participate, try out new words, and receive feedback. If children are to understand the story line in a book, they need to both *listen to* and *discuss* the story. If they are to increase their expressive vocabulary and work toward the decontextualized language of the classroom and books, they have to *use* those words!

One way to promote oral language expression is to engage children in discussion of a story that has been read to them. By asking children questions after story time, you are allowing them time for reflection and giving them the opportunity to practice responding and expressing themselves. However, there are methods and kinds of questions that work best. First, when asking questions about a book it is important to give children time to answer. We have to remember that if we are working with preschoolers they are going to need more time than we do to understand the question and then formulate a response. The optimal wait time is best determined by the child(ren) that you are interacting with, but research suggests that at least three seconds seems to lead to an increase in the number and quality of responses (Rowe, 1972). When asking questions, certain types of questions seem to work better in drawing out children's responses. If the goal is to get children to express themselves, then factual questions or questions where a one-word answer is expected will not do much to encourage oral language expression. A better method is to use open-ended questions. Open-ended questions allow you to "draw a child out" by requesting detail and clarifications and affirming the child's response. This type of questioning also encourages continued discussion of the story (e.g., "Do you think Henny Penny was scared?" "Why do you think Henny Penny was scared?") and mental images and representations of the story line ("What do you think Henny Penny did when the sky started to fall?"). You can "draw the child out" by requesting clarifications and affirming the child's responses. To do this, you can restate, rephrase, summarize, and model (by this we mean *demonstrate*) the use of language. Doing this supports vocabulary and strengthens development of decontextualized language. Open-ended questioning helps to create an environment that encourages complex expressive language *and* enables higher-order thinking.

Examples of open-ended questions that can be used with books include "What's happening in the story?" "What's going on now?" "Why do you think she's unhappy?" "What will happen now?" " How would you feel if you were _____?" To select books that encourage open-ended questions, choose books with rich story structure worth discussing in depth, such as *Blueberries for Sal* by Robert McCloskey, *Tops & Bottoms* by Janet Stevens, *Click, Clack, Moo: Cows That Type* by Doreen Cronin, *Hoodwinked* by Arthur Howard, or *Alexander and the Terrible, Horrible, No Good, Very Bad Day* by Judith Viorst.

Once you choose the book, read ahead and plan where to ask questions (other questions may occur as you are discussing the book, but it is important to be prepared beforehand). There are no "right" questions for the books that you choose; remember that the goal is to get children to discuss the book and use their language skills. Be sure to provide children with plenty of time to come up with their ideas—time to formulate and time to elaborate. Take a pause and listen to their ideas. Be cautious: when children don't come up with good answers, don't give them the answer—go back to the text and read it again to allow them to come up with a new answer. Use pictures sparingly, as the goal is for children to derive meaning from the words alone from *decontextualized language.*

FOSTERING DECONTEXTUALIZED LANGUAGE VIA STORY RECALL

Most of us are familiar with retelling a story. Story recall is predictive of later reading because it demonstrates the ability to listen to and derive meaning from decontextualized language. Many children can tell a story with the support of pictures, but when asked to acquire meaning from words alone, they need practice. Story recall depends on memory of words, the language to express what it is children have understood, and enough background knowledge to make sense of what it is they have been read.

One example of a good title to use for story recall is *One Fine Day* by Nonny Hogrogian, a folktale in which a fox loses his tail to an old woman and then has to bargain to get it back. This book relates a simple story with repetitive language and a clear problem and solution. To illustrate what is happening in the book, you could use a flannel board with just the characters. This basic support allows children to *begin* to retell the story even during the first reading, practicing the action sequence and the language. In addition, the flannel board provides good support for retelling the story later. Retelling from the perspectives of the different characters could also be helpful.

STORY RECALL GOALS

Preschoolers should be able to:

- Retell a familiar story—often with support (some classic examples of stories are the Gingerbread Man, or Goldilocks)
- Create a narrative with two events (i.e., this happened and *then* that happened)
- Discuss books (considering the characters and the story)

By kindergarten children should be able to:

- Listen to a brief story and tell it back in correct sequence, remembering the main characters and using some of the author's language

COMPLEX SENTENCE STRUCTURE

We have been focusing on helping children to understand vocabulary outside of the context provided by pictures. In addition, we have been encouraging you to have children practice saying and talking about new words. The intent should be for children to feel comfortable about speaking up, but also to help them build their language competencies.

Books can assist in encouraging children to produce and understand increasingly complex language. To choose the right book, select books that repeat certain patterns. For example in the book *Lizzy and Skunk* by Marie-Louise Fitzpatrick, the phrases "Lizzy was afraid of ____. But Skunk wasn't" repeat. This keeps the story structure simple, allowing the child resources to formulate longer, more complex sentences. Children practice "retelling" part of the story, using the same phrasing as the book, which is a way to extend their sentence complexity. Provide feedback for children, scaffolding (or supporting) their ability to provide the complete sentence.

COMPLEX SENTENCE STRUCTURE GOALS

Beginning kindergartners should be able to:

- Accurately repeat sentences six to eight words long, keeping the grammatical structure intact
- Speak in (and accurately repeat) sentences five or more words long
- Use verb structures to talk about past and future events, and to make complete questions
- Use some combined clauses with "and," "but," "because"

FOSTERING DECONTEXTUALIZED LANGUAGE USING DIFFERENT GENRES

In addition to selecting books that have increasingly complex sentence structure, choosing books from different genres will also introduce children to diverse language and encourage the understanding and use of decontextualized language. For example, fiction books may have a very different structure and use different language than nonfiction work. Thus, choosing from a variety of different texts will be useful. An engaging nonfiction text on a topic that children are interested in can provide valuable language exposure. Similarly, there are also wonderful books of children's poetry that can be enjoyable to read together and that can foster decontextualized language and also complement many of the skills that we have discussed in other chapters (e.g., rhyming and alliteration). A few suggestions of books of poetry are *Where the Sidewalk Ends* by Shel Silverstein, *Sad Underwear and Other Complications: More Poems for Children and Their Parents* by Judith Viorst, *Joyful Noise: Poems for Two Voices* by Paul Fleischman, *It's Raining Pigs and Noodles* by Jack Prelutsky, and *Hi Koo! A Year of Seasons* by Jon Muth.

RECOMMENDED BOOKS FOR DECONTEXTUALIZED LANGUAGE

Albert the Bear	Nick Butterworth
Click, Clack, Moo: Cows That Type	Doreen Cronin
Lizzy and Skunk	Marie-Louise Fitzpatrick
Joyful Noise: Poems for Two Voices	Paul Fleischman
Corduroy	Don Freeman
One Fine Day	Nonny Hogrogian
Hoodwinked	Arthur Howard
The Growing Story	Ruth Krauss
Blueberries for Sal	Robert McCloskey
Hi Koo! A Year of Seasons	Jon Muth
It's Raining Pigs and Noodles	Jack Prelutsky
Officer Buckle and Gloria	Peggy Rathmann
We're Going on a Bear Hunt	Michael Rosen

The Relatives Came	Cynthia Rylant
Where the Sidewalk Ends	Shel Silverstein
Tops & Bottoms	Janet Stevens
Alexander and the Terrible, Horrible, No Good, Very Bad Day	Judith Viorst
Sad Underwear and Other Complications: More Poems for Children and Their Parents	Judith Viorst
The Bunny Who Found Easter	Charlotte Zolotow

HOW-TO ACTIVITY: Open-Ended Questions

Choose a book to read together, one with rich story structure worth discussing. One example is *Blueberries for Sal* by Robert McCloskey. In *Blueberries for Sal*, a young girl (Sal) is out picking blueberries with her mother. Nearby, a mother bear and her cub are doing the same. Sal and the bear cub get mixed up and follow the wrong mother.

Another good example is *Albert the Bear* by Nick Butterworth. In *Albert the Bear*, Albert joins a group of other toys in a toy shop. The other toys think that Albert is very sad and develop a plan to cheer Albert up. Albert tries to tell them that he isn't sad, it is just the way he looks, but the other toys don't listen. In the end, Albert convinces them that he isn't sad at all.

Examples of open-ended questions for *Blueberries for Sal*:

- Draw the child out by requesting details and clarifications through open-ended questions, such as "What is Sal's family doing?" "What is the bear family doing?"
- Provide children plenty of time to come up with their own ideas—time to formulate answers and time to elaborate on their thoughts.
- Affirm the child's response. For example, respond with "Yes! Sal wandered away from her mother!"
- Encourage continued exploration of the story by asking questions such as "What do you think will happen next?" "Will Sal find her mother?" "Where is the baby bear?"

- Restate, rephrase, and summarize, again modeling (or demonstrating) the language and vocabulary in the book.

Examples of open-ended questions for *Albert the Bear*:

- Ask the children why the other toys think Albert is sad, again giving the them time to provide their answers. You could follow this up by asking them if someone has ever thought that they were feeling something that they weren't.
- Encourage the child to think about, and express, how she would feel if friends didn't listen to her as the other toys didn't listen to Albert. You could model this by explaining a time when this happened to you.
- Ask the child to retell what happened to make Albert really laugh. What was on Albert's face? What makes all the toys laugh?
- You could follow up by asking the child what she thinks is funny and what makes her laugh out loud.

Other good examples are *Click, Clack, Moo: Cows That Type* by Doreen Cronin, *Tops & Bottoms* by Janet Stevens, *Officer Buckle and Gloria* by Peggy Rathmann, and *Hoodwinked* by Arthur Howard.

HOW-TO ACTIVITY: Book Discussion

Children can discuss books!

- Have children identify their favorite book and read the book together.
- Pose and answer specific questions about text (e.g., "Who is Lizzy?" "Why is Lizzy afraid?" when reading *Lizzy and Skunk* by Marie-Louise Fitzpatrick).
- Recite familiar refrains from much-read books, such as "We're going on a bear hunt" (in *We're Going on a Bear Hunt* by Michael Rosen).
- Discuss character motivation and perspective. For example, "Why do you think that Gloria helped Officer Buckle?" (from *Officer Buckle and Gloria* by Peggy Rathmann).

- Have children summarize the story for you (e.g., "What happened in that story?") and tell why they liked it.

REFERENCE

Rowe, Mary Budd. "Wait-Time and Rewards as Instructional Variables: Their Influence on Language, Logic and Fate Control." Paper presented at the Annual Meeting of the National Association for Research on Science Teaching, Chicago, 1972.

BIBLIOGRAPHY

Butterworth, Nick. *Albert the Bear*. Illus. by the author. New York: HarperCollins, 2002. 32 p.

Cronin, Doreen. *Click, Clack, Moo: Cows That Type*. Illus. by Betsy Lewin. New York: Simon & Schuster, 2000. 42 p.

Fitzpatrick, Mary-Louise. *Lizzy and Skunk*. Illus. by the author. New York: DK, 2000. 32 p.

Fleischman, Paul. *Joyful Noise: Poems for Two Voices*. Illus. by Eric Beddows. New York: HarperCollins, 1988. 64 p.

Freeman, Don. *Corduroy*. Illus. by the author. New York: Penguin, 1968. 40 p.

Hogrogian, Nonny. *One Fine Day*. Illus. by the author. New York: Aladdin, 1971. 32 p.

Howard, Arthur. *Hoodwinked*. Illus. by the author. New York: Harcourt, 2001. 36 p.

Krauss, Ruth. *The Growing Story*. Illus. by Helen Oxenbury. New York: Harper-Collins, 1947. 40 p.

McCloskey, Robert. *Blueberries for Sal*. Illus. by the author. New York: Puffin, 1948. 64 p.

Muth, Jon. *Hi Koo! A Year of Seasons*. Illus. by the author. New York: Scholastic, 2014. 32 p.

Prelutsky, Jack. *It's Raining Pigs and Noodles*. Illus. by James Stevenson. New York: Greenwillow, 2005. 160 p.

Rathmann, Peggy. *Officer Buckle and Gloria*. Illus. by the author. New York: Putnam, 1995. 40 p.

Rosen, Michael. *We're Going on a Bear Hunt*. Illus. by Helen Oxenbury. New York: Simon & Schuster, 1989. 36 p.

Rylant, Cynthia. *The Relatives Came*. Illus. by Stephen Gammell. New York: Aladdin, 1985. 32 p.

Silverstein, Shel. *Where the Sidewalk Ends*. Illus. by the author. New York: HarperCollins, 1974. 176 p.

Stevens, Janet. *Tops & Bottoms*. Illus. by the author. San Diego, Calif.: Harcourt, 1995. 40 p.

Viorst, Judith. *Alexander and the Terrible, Horrible, No Good, Very Bad Day*. Illus. by Ray Cruz. New York: Simon & Schuster, 1972. 34 p.

——. *Sad Underwear and Other Complications: More Poems for Children and Their Parents*. Illus. by Richard Hull. New York: Aladdin, 1995. 80 p.

Zolotow, Charlotte. *The Bunny Who Found Easter*. Illus. by Helen Craig. New York: Houghton Mifflin, 1959. 32 p.

8

WRITING

You can make anything by writing.

—C. S. Lewis

Our emphasis in this book has been on speaking and reading to children to support emerging literacy. In addition, there are also many good reasons to *write* with young children. As children develop, reading and writing should go hand in hand. They are reciprocal processes: reading is taking the printed word and converting it to sounds; writing is taking the sounds and converting them to the printed word. It is obvious, then, that reading and writing together fuel emerging literacy. As with the other skills discussed in this book, the types of activities that you choose to focus on will depend on the age and developmental level of the child. For example, a three-year-old who is just learning to recognize letters (and may not yet have good fine motor control) may not be ready to start writing independently. However, this child could benefit from practicing writing letters by copying or tracing examples you have produced. On the other hand, an older child may be ready to start "writing" his or her own words and sentences. As we have mentioned frequently, it is also important to engage multiple modes of interacting and allow ample practice as children learn new skills. Incorporating writing with some of the reading activities already discussed will help to reinforce new literacy skills. This chapter will explore the benefits writing confers to the development of reading with some of the skills discussed in previous chapters and will also help you to understand what to expect when children begin writing and spelling on their own.

HOW WILL WRITING AND SPELLING ENCOURAGE THE DEVELOPMENT OF READING SKILLS?

To start, writing with young children will improve their *concepts about print* and *alphabet knowledge*, by demonstrating that it is the words (and letters) on the pages that contain the message and not the pictures. We want to encourage young children to differentiate between pictures, numbers, and letters; and having them write the letters they know, in addition to reading those letters, can help with this. As their literacy emerges, writing can strengthen *phonological awareness* by helping children to understand the alphabetic principle, introduced in chapter 5. That is, through writing, children come to directly understand that we use letters and letter patterns to represent the sounds of spoken language. In this way, writing gives letters

"meaning" for children. Writing can also encourage *vocabulary* development by encouraging children to use the new words they are learning in
their own writing, whether it is as simple as writing a list of vegetable names
they have learned from a book like *Tops & Bottoms* by Janet Stevens, to
incorporating a new word in their own story writing. Additionally, writing
can encourage the development of *decontextualized language* that is used
in books. Writing their own stories (or dictating them to you) can encourage narrative skill and help to make the structure of stories as told in books
more concrete. Finally, by writing letters and words that are important to
children, such as those in their own, family members', or pets' names, we
inspire a drive toward literacy. Through actively writing words as well as
reading them, children become invested in learning how to communicate
through reading *and* writing.

WHAT IS THE DEVELOPMENTAL PROGRESSION
OF WRITING AND SPELLING?

As mentioned in chapter 1, even children as young as two or three may
show an interest in writing. While their early writing may look like mere
scribbles, by about age three those scribbles may begin to look more like
letters. So, as children develop, their scribbles will begin to include some
familiar letters (and probably numbers as well). When beginning to write
and spell words on their own, children will focus on the most salient or
"loudest" sound (the sounds that are the most forcefully articulated or
stressed) in a word, writing just the letter *s* for *mouse*, or *n* for *and*. If children know how to write their letters, their invented spelling will reflect
their degree of phonemic awareness. For example, if a child intends to
write, "I like housekeeping," you might get an initial response that looks
like "IKSKP," with no word boundaries. Alternatively (and over time) a
child might write a response that uses a more alphabetic spelling with word
boundaries like this: "I elk hskpen." The image at the beginning of this
chapter demonstrates another example of this latter type and, along with
the writing, indicates that the child writing the message likes butterflies. As
children continue to progress, their writing will use more alphabetic principles as they reach a more mature reading and writing level.

ACTIVITIES TO SUPPORT WRITING

Name writing is one of the easiest ways to get children to begin to understand the process of matching letters and sounds. As we know, a child's name is very special to him or her and being able to write one's name is a landmark achievement. Encourage children to write their first names, and for children who have mastered this, you could have them write their last names. A good book to go along with this activity (that also introduces the idea of different writing systems) is *Yoko Writes Her Name* by Rosemary Wells.

Interactive writing involves having the child come up with a brief message, list, or letter. You can then write the message on an easel, whiteboard, or piece of paper, showing letter by letter, the letters that create a given word. Children can then illustrate their messages with pictures. Over time, children can begin to take on writing more of the words on their own.

Invented spelling, or writing down words as they sound, is an outstanding way for young children (roughly four- to six-year-olds) to practice focusing on phoneme awareness. In invented spelling the child attempts to write a response to a question or prompt on her own, using what she knows about sounds, letters, and sight words to guide her. You may choose to go over the writing with the child to "translate" or explain her invented spelling, but you should encourage the child's invented spellings. As adults, we often want to make sure that children spell words correctly. And while we do want to work toward correct conventional spelling, the child's own invented spellings are also very useful. It shows that the child is actively trying to sound out the word and match it up with the written letters. While children might not always get it right at first, allowing them to make mistakes will help them to work toward correct spellings.

Writing independently. As children develop, allowing them any opportunity to practice writing or spelling is valuable. Give them access to scrap paper and any kind of writing tool, such as crayons, pencils, or pens. Encourage them to write whatever they want. This could be as simple as a grocery list like the characters in *Bunny Cakes* by Rosemary Wells or a list of what they want for their birthday or Christmas. Have them write a letter to a friend or relative and help them to mail it. Giving your child a writing journal (which can be a simple notebook they decorate with stickers) and a fancy pen or pencil will show them that writing is special or important. An older child might be interested in "publishing" his or her own book. This can be easily achieved by stapling together some plain paper and having the child write and illustrate his or her story. A good book to read to a child interested in writing on his or her own is *The Best Story* by Eileen Spinelli. This is a book about a girl who has entered a writing contest to win a roller-coaster ride and the difficulties she has writing until she discovers that the best story is her own. Again, anything that encourages the child to write and spell will support emerging literacy.

RECOMMENDED BOOKS FOR WRITING

Click, Clack, Moo: Cows That Type	Doreen Cronin
Hoodwinked	Arthur Howard
A Letter to Amy	Ezra Jack Keats
Office Buckle and Gloria	Peggy Rathmann
The Best Story	Eileen Spinelli
Tops & Bottoms	Janet Stevens
Bunny Cakes	Rosemary Wells
Yoko Writes Her Name	Rosemary Wells

HOW-TO ACTIVITY:
Writing (Developing Concepts about Print)

Have children create (or dictate):

A letter making a demand (as in *Click, Clack, Moo: Cows That Type*)

OR

A list of safety tips (as in *Officer Buckle and Gloria*)

OR

Labels for pictures of thematic vocabulary (as in *Tops & Bottoms*)

HOW-TO ACTIVITY: Writing (Building Vocabulary)

Using the book Hoodwinked *by Arthur Howard*
This book describes a young witch girl's quest for the perfect pet, using many adjectives.
Children can produce adjectives for their ideal pet. You can then write down or have the children write the adjectives; next, the children can illustrate a picture of their "ideal" pet.

HOW-TO ACTIVITY:
Writing (Building on Invented Spellings and Vocabulary)

Post Office: Using the Book A Letter to Amy *by Ezra Jack Keats*
This is a fun activity for children who are beginning to be able to write more independently. First, read *A Letter to Amy* by Ezra Jack Keats and talk about the process of writing a letter and the basic format that is used.
Then, in a corner of the preschool or day-care setting (or even at home), you can set up a post office area, providing children with paper, pens and pencils, stickers to use as stamps, and envelopes recycled from junk mail to mail their messages to friends or siblings. Reading and responding to the messages they have received will also give children the chance to practice their newly developing skills. You could even have children take turns delivering the mail (either to small mailboxes you have for each child or to the child directly) thus encouraging children to learn to read and recognize the names of other children.

BIBLIOGRAPHY

Cronin, Doreen. *Click, Clack, Moo: Cows That Type.* Illus. by Betsy Lewin. New York: Simon & Schuster, 2000. 42 p.

Howard, Arthur. *Hoodwinked.* Illus. by the author. New York: Harcourt, 2001. 36 p.

Keats, Ezra Jack. *A Letter to Amy.* Illus. by the author. New York: Penguin, 1968. 32 p.

Rathmann, Peggy. *Officer Buckle and Gloria*. Illus. by the author. New York: Putnam, 1995. 40 p.

Spinelli, Eileen. *The Best Story*. Illus. by Anne Wilsdorf. New York: Penguin, 2008. 32 p.

Stevens, Janet. *Tops & Bottoms*. Illus. by the author. San Diego, Calif.: Harcourt, 1995. 40 p.

Wells, Rosemary. *Bunny Cakes*. Illus. by the author. New York: Penguin, 1997. 32 p.

——. *Yoko Writes Her Name*. Illus. by the author. New York: Hyperion, 2008. 32 p.

ONLINE RESOURCES RELATED TO EARLY LITERACY AND READING

BARBARA BUSH FOUNDATION

The mission of the Barbara Bush Foundation is to establish literacy as a value in every home in America.

http://www.barbarabushfoundation.com

BETWEEN THE LIONS

Between the Lions is a PBS children's show designed to help children learn to read. This site offers stories, games, and video clips to promote literacy.

http://pbskids.org/lions/

BOOK ADVENTURE

Book Adventure is for children K–8. Children can download books to read offline and then come back the site to take quizzes on what they have read. Children demonstrate their comprehension of books and can earn rewards for reading.

http://www.bookadventure.com

BOOKSHARE

Bookshare is the world's largest accessible digital library for people with print and learning disabilities (such as dyslexia). Membership is free for individuals (with proof of disability) and provides access to thousands of digital books.

https://www.bookshare.org

DOLLY PARTON'S IMAGINATION LIBRARY

An organization created by Dolly Parton to help provide books to preschool children and their families to encourage early literacy and excitement about reading.

http://www.imaginationlibrary.com

DYSLEXIA FOUNDATION

The Dyslexia Foundation (TDF) is an organization established to help identify and assist children with dyslexia.

http://dyslexiafoundation.org

EZRA JACK KEATS FOUNDATION

Author Ezra Jack Keats (*The Snowy Day* and *A Letter to Amy*, among many others) was dedicated to children's literacy. This website has resources that will support children's literacy including valuable information for parents, educators, and librarians. There are also games and activities for children tied to the characters in Keats's stories.

http://www.ezra-jack-keats.org

FIRST BOOK

First Book provides access to new books for children in need. To receive free books you must register with the site and meet certain eligibility requirements.

http://www.firstbook.org

GET READY TO READ

Resources for parents and early childhood educators. Early literacy activities for children.

http://www.getreadytoread.org

GIGGLE POETRY

A fun way to expose children to different writing styles. This site has hundreds of poems available to read online.

http://www.gigglepoetry.com

GUYS READ

A website dedicated to motivating young boys to read. The site was founded by author and first national ambassador of young people's literature Jon Scieszka. The site provides reading recommendations for boys of all ages.

http://www.guysread.com

INTERNATIONAL CHILDREN'S DIGITAL LIBRARY

An online library whose goal is to collect and make available the best historical and contemporary children's books from around the world, in their original language.

http://en.childrenslibrary.org

INTERNATIONAL DYSLEXIA ASSOCIATION

The IDA provides information and services for individuals with dyslexia and other reading and writing difficulties.

http://www.interdys.org

INTERNATIONAL READING ASSOCIATION

The International Reading Association is a professional membership dedicated to literacy and reading instruction. The website provides useful resources for parents, caregivers, teachers, librarians, and more.

http://www.reading.org

KIDSREADS

Kidsreads provides book recommendations and reviews of children's books.

http://www.kidsreads.com

LITERACY HOW

Literacy How is an organization whose mission is to train teachers in the science of reading. The website offers valuable resources for educators, parents, and caregivers.

http://www.literacyhow.com

MIGHTY BOOK

Free books, music, and songs to help children learn to read.

http://www.mightybook.com

NATIONAL CENTER FOR LEARNING DISABILITIES

The National Center for Learning Disabilities (NCLD) is an organization that works to support children, adolescents, and adults with learning disabilities. The site has useful resources for parents and professionals.

http://www.ncld.org

NATIONAL JEWISH COALITION FOR LITERACY

The National Jewish Coalition for Literacy is a coalition of national Jewish agencies and organizations committed to help all of America's children learn to read by the end of third grade.

http://www.njcl.net/njcl/Home.html

RAISING A READER

A program to promote early literacy and to help families establish reading routines in their homes.

http://www.raisingareader.org

REACH OUT AND READ

Reach Out and Read is organization founded by pediatricians to promote early literacy and school readiness. Their mission is to encourage parents to read aloud to their children and to provide parents with books.

http://www.reachoutandread.org

READ TO GROW

Read to Grow is an organization that aims to support language development and literacy beginning in infancy. The site provides links to many resources for parents and caregivers.

https://www.readtogrow.org

READ TO ME

The Read to Me program is designed to promote early literacy by providing reading resources for parents and to encourage young moms and dads to read to their children. The website has many resources including hands-on activities and book suggestions for parents of infants and young toddlers.

http://readtomeprogram.org

READING IS FUNDAMENTAL

The mission of RIF is to motivate young children to read by making reading fun. The website provides lots of reading resources including book lists, activities, and more.

http://www.rif.org

READING ROCKETS

Information, lessons, strategies, and activities for parents and teachers to help young children learn to read.

http://www.readingrockets.org

READWRITETHINK

The goal of ReadWriteThink is to give parents, caregivers, and teachers access to resources related to reading and language arts. The website offers many free materials for children from kindergarten through high school.

http://www.readwritethink.org

STARFALL

The Starfall learn-to-read website encourages early literacy skills including phonemic awareness through fun games, videos, and stories. It is designed primarily for children from pre-K through second grade.

http://www.starfall.com

STORYBIRD

This website is a wonderful tool to encourage children to write their own stories. The site provides children with access to digital artwork they can incorporate into the books that they create. The site also offers access to free books.

http://storybird.com

STORYLINE ONLINE

This website has videos of actors and actresses reading popular children's books aloud. Children can listen to the story and see the pictures in the book as it is being read.

http://www.storylineonline.net

STORYPLACE

StoryPlace is a digital library for young children (preschool through elementary school) that provides activities and reading suggestions. The site has both an English and a Spanish version.

http://www.storyplace.org

STUDYDOG

StudyDog is an early reading (pre-K through second grade) computer-based program. The program is research based and focuses on many of the skills discussed in our book, along with skills necessary for older children. The program is tailored for the progress of each child and teaches skills in a fun and engaging way.

http://www.studydog.com

VOKI

Voki allows children to design an avatar who can then be programmed to speak using the child's voice. The site can be a useful tool to encourage writing. Children can type in what they want their avatar to say and the character will read what they have written.

http://www.voki.com

WE GIVE BOOKS

This website is owned by Pearson Foundation, and has hundreds of e-books available for children to read for free. The site allows you to search and sort the books by age, author, genre, and more.

http://www.wegivebooks.org

ZERO TO THREE

Zero to Three is the nation's leading resource on the first three years of life. The site includes useful information about early development, covering areas such as language, literacy, and school readiness.

http://www.zerotothree.org

INDEX

ABOUT THE AUTHORS

Julia Irwin is a senior research scientist at Haskins Laboratories in New Haven, Connecticut, a not-for-profit research institution with a focus on communication, language, and reading. Dr. Irwin is also an associate professor in the Department of Psychology at Southern Connecticut State University.

Dina Moore is an associate professor in the Department of Psychology at Southern Connecticut State University and a research affiliate of Haskins Laboratories. Her research examines individual differences in reading skill and the cognitive factors that underlie these differences.

"This is my best Christmas present ever," said Great-Aunt Harriet.

Franklin got that good-all-over feeling one more time.

Great-Aunt Harriet unwrapped her gift slowly and carefully.

Inside was a play, written by Franklin and dedicated to her.

On Christmas Eve, Great-Aunt Harriet
came to visit and Franklin was allowed to
open her present.

He ripped off the paper.

"It's perfect!" said Franklin. "Thank you."

Great-Aunt Harriet beamed. She had
made a stage for Franklin's puppet shows.

"Now open yours," Franklin insisted.

The next morning, Franklin put his present
on top of the collection box.

Then Franklin and his friends hauled the
box to the big tree at the Town Hall.

They placed each present under the tree.

Franklin knew he would miss his marble
collection. Still, he didn't feel at all sad. Instead,
he felt good all over.

Franklin played with his puppets and thought about how Great-Aunt Harriet chose her gifts.

"The best presents are special to give and to receive," he whispered.

Then Franklin saw his marble collection and he knew that the marbles were special enough for the toy drive.

Franklin polished them and put them into a soft purple bag.

He wrapped the present and made a gift tag that read:

These are lucky marbles.
Merry Christmas.

Franklin raced home after school and looked through his toys again.

Somebody else might love Elephant, but she was worn from so much hugging.

And Franklin wasn't sure that the red car went fast enough.

Franklin was upset. At first, all of his toys had seemed too special to give away. Now, nothing seemed special enough.

The next day at school, the collection box was brimming.

"You've all been very generous," said Mr. Owl. "Do you know that your gift might be the only one somebody receives this holiday?"

Franklin gulped. He'd never thought of that. He had to bring a present tomorrow!

Franklin squeezed the present and shook it.

"No peeking," laughed his mother.

"Do you know what it is?" asked Franklin eagerly.

"It must be something special." His mother smiled. "Great-Aunt Harriet always gives presents that mean something to you and to her."

"Like last year," said Franklin.

Great-Aunt Harriet knew that he loved to put on plays. And she gave him two puppets that had been hers when she was little. It was one of Franklin's best presents ever.

When Franklin got home, there was a gift for him under the tree. It was from Great-Aunt Harriet.

Franklin was so excited that he forgot all about choosing a gift for the toy drive.

But Franklin was too busy to think about the toy drive.

He played the recorder in the school concert, made a card for Mr. Owl and wrote a holiday story.

"I'll pick a toy after school," he promised himself.

The next day at school, Franklin asked his friends what they were giving.

Beaver was donating her big book of questions and answers.

"I already know all the answers," she boasted.

"I'm giving a puzzle," said Bear. "I only did it once."

Franklin frowned. "I'm giving a truck ... I think."

He had two days left to decide.

Franklin asked his father to help him fix the truck.

"We can try," said his father. "But it won't look new or even gently used."

"It's all I have. Everything else is too special to give away."

"I'd like you to think about that," said Franklin's father. "Christmas is a time to be generous."

Then Franklin found his best green marble. It had
been missing for weeks.

"Fantastic!" he shouted.

Franklin loved his marbles. He had won every
marble in his collection, and each one was beautiful.

Franklin picked through the rest of the toys.
He decided to keep everything but a rusty truck with
a missing wheel.

That evening Franklin dug through his toys.
He picked up a shiny red car.

"I remember this," he said, wheeling it around.
"Vroom!"

Next, Franklin pulled out a stuffed elephant
and held her tight.

"I wondered where you'd gone!" he cried.

Every December the students in Mr. Owl's class donated toys for needy families. The toys could be new or carefully used.

When Mr. Owl put out the collection box, everyone was excited. They had three days to choose the perfect gifts to give.

For Hannah and Charlotte Cowan,
two very special girls — P.B.

To my parents, for the warm Christmas memories — B.C.

Franklin

Franklin is a trademark of Kids Can Press Ltd.

Text © 1998 Contextx Inc.
Illustrations © 1998 Brenda Clark Illustrator Inc.

Interior illustrations prepared with the assistance of Shelley Southern.

Kids Can Press acknowledges the financial support of the Ontario
Arts Council; the Canada Council for the Arts and the Government
of Canada, through the CBF, for our publishing activity.

Published in Canada by
Kids Can Press Ltd.
25 Dockside Drive
Toronto, ON M5A 0B5

Published in the U.S. by
Kids Can Press Ltd.
2250 Military Road
Tonawanda, NY 14150

www.kidscanpress.com

The hardcover edition of this book is smyth sewn casebound.
The paperback edition of this book is limp sewn with a drawn-on cover.
Manufactured in Buji, Shenzhen, China, in 3/2013 by WKT Company

CM 98 0 9 8 7 6 5 4 3
CDN PA 97 0 9 8 7 6 5 4
CMC PA 13 0 9 8 7 6 5 4 3 2 1

Library and Archives Canada Cataloguing in Publication

Bourgeois, Paulette
   Franklin's Christmas gift / written by Paulette Bourgeois ;
illustrated by Brenda Clark.

(A classic Franklin story)
ISBN 978-1-77138-001-0

   1. Franklin (Fictitious character : Bourgeois) – Juvenile fiction.
I. Clark, Brenda II. Title. III. Series: Classic Franklin story

PS8553.O85477F84 2013   jC813'.54   C2012-907882-4

Kids Can Press is a *corus*™ Entertainment company

Franklin's Christmas Gift

FRANKLIN loved Christmas. He could name all of Santa's reindeer. He could tie ribbons into bows and play "Silent Night" on his recorder.

Franklin liked to give presents and to receive them. But this year he couldn't decide what to give to the Christmas toy drive.

Franklin's Christmas Gift

Written by Paulette Bourgeois
Illustrated by Brenda Clark

Kids Can Press